Praise for Eric Butterworth

"The Creative Life *arrived the very day I needed it. Eric Butterworth arrived in my life the very year I needed him. He has been, is now, and shall forever be my teacher.*"

—MAYA ANGELOU

"*Eric Butterworth is a humble, soft-spoken drum major of truth and one of the greatest minds of our time. With simple yet profound insight, he touches our hearts, expands our minds, and transforms our lives. Gifted with the uncanny ability to reach the deepest fibers of our souls with his pen, Butterworth takes us on a journey within to explore every aspect of our spiritual lives.*"

—LES BROWN, author of *Live Your Dreams*

"*Eric Butterworth has done it again, proving why he is one of the most brilliant and respected metaphysical teachers of our time. Anyone reading his book can use his practical steps, guided imagery, and mental exercises to awaken the sleeping creative genius within and achieve greatness.*"

—TERRY COLE-WHITTAKER, author of *Dare to Be Great!*

"*Life-changing insights from one of our greatest living teachers. I respect Eric Butterworth enormously.*"

—DR. WAYNE W. DYER, author of *Wisdom of the Ages*

"*Want to find and release your creative flow? The steps are here in Eric Butterworth's* The Creative Life. *The door to your highest self will open once you are bold enough to knock. Please read this book.*"

—JAMES REDFIELD, author of *The Celestine Prophecy* and *The Secret of Shambhala*

"The Creative Life *is simply a blessing. With luminous clarity and unparalleled understanding of New Thought principles, Eric Butterworth offers the gift of his own genius. To learn how to express your unique and matchless creativity, buy this book, and read it again and again. You will treasure it forever.*"

—MARY MANIN MORRISSEY, author of *Building Your Field of Dreams*

The Creative Life

•

SEVEN KEYS TO YOUR INNER GENIUS

Eric Butterworth

JEREMY P. TARCHER/PUTNAM
a member of Penguin Group (USA) Inc.
New York

Most Tarcher/Putnam books are available at special quantity discounts for bulk purchase for sales promotions, premiums, fund-raising, and educational needs. Special books or book excerpts also can be created to fit specific needs. For details, write Penguin Group (USA) Inc. Special Markets, 375 Hudson Street, New York, NY 10014.

Jeremy P. Tarcher/Putnam
a member of
Penguin Group (USA) Inc.
375 Hudson Street
New York, NY 10014
www. penguin.com

New Thought Library Series Publisher: Joel Fotinos
First trade paperback edition 2003

The Library of Congress catalogued the hardcover edition as follows:

Butterworth, Eric.
The creative life : seven keys to your inner genius / Eric Butterworth.
p.   cm.
ISBN 1-58542-094-8
1. Creative ability—Religious aspects—Christianity.
2. Bible. O.T. Genesis I:1–II:3—Criticism,
interpretation, etc.   I. Title.
BT709.5.B88   2001   2001018913
248.4'8997—dc21

ISBN 1-58542-270-3 (paperback edition)

Printed in the United States of America

1   3   5   7   9   10   8   6   4   2

Book design by Jennifer Ann Daddio

ACKNOWLEDGMENTS

To Dr. Peter J. D'Adamo, for his persistent encouragement to write this book.

To those literary giants of the ages, who have ignited in me the sparks of Oneness, and who have become *my gurus*.

To my mother, who influenced my life more than she knew by patiently allowing me to dream, and by her faith in my faith to make real the most impossible dreams.

To Olga, my faithful, loving partner and caregiver, who has redefined what it means to be a wife. She is the best student I have had in over fifty years of teaching Truth, and she holds me editorially to an absolute metaphysical ideal that we have set together and which is reflected in this book.

To the multitudes of Truth seekers who walk in darkness due to a primitive perception of the creation, to minds open and hearts receptive to a "larger thought of God" and a new insight into the Superconscious flow from within.

To the vision held by an increasing number of people of a planet earth blessed with the energy potential of peace among men.

All scripture quotations are from the American Standard Version of the Bible unless otherwise cited.

CONTENTS

FOREWORD

"Woe to the book you can read without constantly wondering about the author!" wrote the Rumanian mystic E. M. Cioran.

In his new book *The Creative Life*, Eric Butterworth has produced a guide to the mysterious power of the hidden side of things. By employing the primordial and beautiful "Seven Days of Creation" metaphor, he draws a parallel between that first emergence of light from darkness and our own emergence into a more creative and useful life.

The sheer conceptual scale of this work can be

perhaps best appreciated by a quick study of the book's beginning and end.

The Creative Life opens with an examination of light. To Eric Butterworth, illumination and creativity are linked by a magical moment sometimes known as the "Eureka Act," the sudden shaking together of two previously unconnected ways of linking thoughts together. Interestingly, it is here that the author sees a role for prayer. "It is prayer that helps to recenter ourselves in that inner light," he writes, and he is quick to remind us that we are not mere supplicants: "We do not pray to God; we pray from the consciousness of God." Prayer is not simply a ray of light coming downward as so commonly depicted, but rather a beam of creative thought that radiates outward and upward as well.

The book ends with a discussion of the "Creative Intermission" (the day of rest alluded to in Genesis), which for Eric Butterworth is about natural rhythms and cycles. These rhythms are not artificially created ornaments of enforced idleness but rather part of a deep underground matrix, one which makes its presence felt in sleep and sleep-like states, dreams, and fantasy. The whole evidence indicates that its origins go back to primitive, infantile forms of thought. To the author, this is the time for self-evaluation, and I found it interesting to reflect on just how much contemporary psychoanalysis takes place inside this realm.

As with all of Eric Butterworth's works, *The Creative Life* is realized with a rare combination of lucidity, gentleness, and enthusiasm—the last a special characteristic of the author, signifying *en theos*—a god within.

"Happy is he who bears a god within," wrote Louis Pasteur, "an ideal of beauty and who obeys it, an ideal of art, of science. All are lighted by a reflection of the infinite." That is why I think *The Creative Life* is so important, and why I am certain that you will wonder about its author. Eric Butterworth's enthusiasm is truly the work of a "god within" who has blessed him with the ways and means to say those essential things that are inside him.

The fundamental message of this book is quite simple. Like God, our creative powers are infinite. The art of the book resides in the manner by which we as readers move toward that simple realization: Eric Butterworth's accomplished weaving of the infinite, the ephemeral, and the ineffable into a fabric of thought and action that we can use to clothe our souls.

—*Dr. Peter J. D'Adamo*

PROLOGUE

The most remarkable development of the past century is the Internet. Its development reveals the creative genius of *Homo sapiens* at its finest, and it's capable of linking together unbelievable amounts of knowledge. Perhaps the closest parallel is the mind of God.

Anyone may access the Internet and have the wisdom of civilization at his or her fingertips. And, although it may be a stretch for your religious beliefs, I am here to say that anyone may access the mind of God and realize the answers to all of his or her needs.

As Emerson said, "Every person is an inlet and may become an outlet to all there is in God."

The Creative Life is a book about you, your transcendent self, your infinite potential, your inner genius. In it we are going to look at the seven days of creation, which are presented in the controversial first chapter of Genesis and on which the whole Bible rests.

I should make it clear that my first priority is not to teach the Bible. Rather it is to teach the underlying message as it pertains to your life today. Through a vital, metaphysical interpretation, we will come to see the seven days of creation as a treasure map that holds the seven keys to unlocking your creative genius.

Consequently, before I go any further, I should say a few words about the Bible. Most people have a Bible as something to swear on, to record births and marriages in, and to display on a family altar. The scripture it contains is treated as a record of accomplishments of an anthropomorphic deity. However, I do not feel the creation story was ever intended to be considered in this way. In fact, I feel this interpretation does the reader a profound disservice. Philosophers through the ages have always said that man has but to know himself to discover the secrets of the universe. Is there any better tool for understanding the self and discovering the secrets of the universe than the Bible? It is the finest mirror of life, a mirror in which we can receive the most revealing insights into ourselves. But there is no mirror effect if we read it as an historically true, literal document. To study it in this way is to reduce its importance to our understanding of ourselves and the world around us.

And the world around us today is crying out for our creative genius, yours and mine. For each of us has the ability to set the world afire! I know this to be true. It is my hope that when you have finished *The Creative Life*, you too will know that you are one of the great co-creators, thinkers, and do-ers of our age and that you will be joyful, for mystic thinkers have always seen the world as a shadow of a great reality. They have observed with Elizabeth Barrett Browning, "Earth is crammed with heaven, and every common bush afire with God, but only he who sees takes off his shoes, the rest sit round it and pluck blackberries."

The creation story is not something God does or did: It is what God *is*. It is a process within the Principle acting on itself. Creativity is the God process in you, expressing as you. The creation is your story, the key to your creative genius.

The Creative Life

INTRODUCTION

I like to think that the origin of this book was the same impulse that has guided so many creative beings to produce their masterpieces: the desire to give tangible form to the knowledge that we are all one with God. The aim of *The Creative Life* is to allow you to access these same impulses in yourself—if they are not already manifest—or to inspire you to still greater manifestations of your own creative genius. It is my belief that when you are finished reading this book you will realize that you are no less creative than God Himself.

How did I come to choose the seven days as a metaphor for the book? To me, the seven days of creation outline in a metaphysical sense the important keys to the release of one's creative genius. For although creationists insist that the world was created in seven days 6,000 years ago, I do not feel the creation story was ever intended as history. The authors of the Bible were essentially poets who used symbolic words and forms. A similar example can be found in Shakespeare's writing about the forest of Arden; in it one could find "tongues in trees, books in the running brooks, sermons in stones, and good in everything."

Thus I avoid dogmatic or generalized interpretations of the Bible even in a metaphysical sense. I encourage you not to look to it for *meaning*, but instead to think of it as something that simply *is*. As a teacher I fail you if I claim to give you *the* interpretation of it. But you can find the meaning in it by dealing with it at the level of your need, and with the insights revealed to you by your inner flow of inspiration.

This, then, is what I believe the creation story is about. Spirit being you. *Br'esheth Elohim.* In the beginning, God. Too often we think of creativity in terms of something that has form and substance. We talk of inventors, artists, writers, and designers, as "creative people." We say wistfully, "I wish I were creative." The fact is that everyone is creative. It is the one supreme fact of existence. It is the nature of the Infinite to create, and it is the nature of each person to be creative. This, then, is the creative process that Genesis articulates. Creation is not something that God does, or did. It is what God is. It is what you are.

As we discern this inner meaning of the seven days of creation, it is also my hope that you will begin to see creativity not as a series of discrete facts but as a moving process, like the opening of a rose. If we were to use lapse-time photography, we could break it down into seven unique pictures. Since we are using words, we will refer to them as seven keys, seven keys to the release of your creative process in the discovery of your own, internal, creative genius.

If what you are thinking right now is, "That's all well and good, but I would really like to have something to show for all this at the end of the day, then I would ask you—for the purposes of the swift unlocking of your genius—to think of creativity for the time being as an "Aha!" It could be likened to Einstein meditating on a scientific problem and suddenly saying, "Aha! I have it." What did he have? Nothing. Nothing had been physically created; he simply had the vision of a universal law that would enable humankind reach a higher level of light. He had a change in his mind-set.

This, then, is the goal of *The Creative Life:* to change your mind-set. To allow you to *know* that you are one with God and that all your works are good.

ONE

•

Let There Be Light

•

And God said, "Let There be Light,"
and there was light.

We are living today in a complex and changing world. If there is one thing needed more than anything else, it is light. Light in terms of insight into ourselves, guidance along life's way, knowledge of the "secrets of the universe," and the wisdom to use this light and not abuse it.

The clearest thinkers the race has produced have always seen the course of their lives as the quest for light. Goethe, who spent his life on this quest, gasped on his deathbed the words "Light, more light." He knew instinctively that death is not a journey into the darkness, but a journey through the darkness into the light, the brief drifting of a cloud across the road we are traveling on through which we pass from sunlight to sunlight.

Too often, however, the search for light is "out there" in institutions and holy places and great books and the influence of master teachers. Like the absent-minded professor who searches high and low for his glasses, only to discover that he has been wearing them all the time, we need to realize that we are always looking through God-colored glasses. The illumination we seek, the knowledge of God in ourselves is within us, but, like the professor, we tend to look everywhere except within our own consciousness for that Truth.

Many people avoid the word *illumination* because, for them, it has connotations of the supernatural. Others avoid it because they think illumination can only be experienced by an elite illuminati of masters or gurus, favored ones gifted with spiritual insight. It is true that highly advanced souls do experience a deep awareness of cosmic light, but every person can experience illumination.

How can this become so for you? It will become true when you realize that you and God are inextricably linked in a mission of co-creation, when you surrender to the idea that even as a wave is the ocean expressing as a wave, so you are the Allness of God expressing as you.

"In the Beginning, God Created . . ."

This phrase would seem to mean first in order of time. In fact, that is an error. It should be "first in order of creation." "In the beginning" *(B'resheth Elohim)* means, in principle, Allness, omnipresence, one power, one elemental energy, One Mind. Creation is not something God does or did, it is what God is. It is what you are.

Wherever Spirit is at all, the whole of Spirit must be. And because Spirit is omnipresent, the whole of Spirit is present at every point in space at the same time. This calls for a larger concept of God than most people have allowed for. It means that whatever your need, the whole of Spirit is present in the need—all of mind, the whole of healing life, all of substance, all of love.

So when God says "Let there be light," it does not connote a tiny beam of light energy flowing into your life. It means the whole of God-light present in its entirety at the point where you are. When Jesus said, "I am the light of the world," he was not referring to himself. He was pointing to the "I Am," the divine flame that you experience at the point of your

I AMness. When he goes on to say, "You are the light of the world. . . . Let your light shine," he is not referring to an illumination that comes to us from without. He is talking about an inner illumination—an inner revelation, acknowledgment, acceptance, identification by us of our ever-present light within.

How Can We Access This Light?

Prayer is the experience of recentering ourselves in that inner light, then becoming a transparency for its radiance. In doing so, it behooves us to remember, we do not pray *to* God, we pray *from* the consciousness *of* God.

You may have to recondition your whole perception of life to grasp this point. It is important for you to meditate on this idea until it becomes a part of you.

Meister Eckhart was aware of the very human tendency to be dominated by an objective perspective of

God, an anthropomorphic God who rules over our lives with an iron hand. To change his way of thinking, he made what could be considered the most startling statement in the history of religion when he confessed that he boldly "prayed God to rid me of God."

What did he mean by this? I believe he meant that if we are dominated by a God who is "out there" we will always be restricted in our prayer's effectiveness. God is not a person to whom we should pray, but a spirit by which we should live. Emerson said, "When we have broken with the God of tradition, and ceased from the God of the intellect, then God fires us with his presence." What is this fire? The outstreaming of light, of creativity.

One Mind, Divine Mind

You are creative because you are an expression of Divine Mind. There is no such thing as a person who is not creative. People who believe this are those who think that creativity must manifest itself in a certain way. The thing you must realize is that it does not matter whether this creativity is engaged in solving a math problem, creating a revolutionary microchip, putting together inspiring words and phrases, or combining lovely melodies and chord progressions to compose great music. Beethoven, Michelangelo, Edison, Shakespeare—anyone who has ever been called a great master was a conduit of enlightenment. It is just that in each case the medium changed. The process for each is exactly the same: you and God working as co-creators to manifest His light.

Another illustration: A number of people could come together in a group meditation, each one seeking "Light . . . more light." Sitting together in one room, each could get centered in the One Mind. Then each could focus their thoughts on the source of light within them and let the creative intention that is right for them reveal itself. Out of this flow of radiant, pure light one could write a poem, another could paint a garden scene, another could design a building, another could compose a sonata, and another could come up with an advertising campaign. Each has touched the same Mind, but each expressed it according to their needs and at the level of their consciousness.

As Emerson said, "There is one mind common to all individual minds." Just as the acorn has a need to become an oak tree and the grape seed has a need to become the grapevine, so you will draw out of the Divine Mind whatever is necessary for your needs.

And the earth was without form and void,
and darkness was upon the face of the deep.

This is a challenging statement—a challenge to us to get away from the delusion of outer lights, to get back to the "true light that lighteth every person coming into the world." It calls us to "enter into the inner chamber and close the door." The deep is the wise silence within us, beyond sight and sound, beyond sensation and materiality.

It is primal illumination. Just knowing.

Jesus said, "Take my yoke upon you and learn of me, for my yoke is easy and my burden is light." This is a different connotation of the word *light* from the one we generally imagine. But consider that the word "yoke" means union or oneness, so Jesus is saying when you are centered in your own oneness in the Divine Mind, you walk in light, you live in light, and you see every challenge or burden *from* that light. He is saying that if you know your oneness in the universe, as I do, you will experience the same inner light and outer power that I manifest.

In his book *Talks With Great Composers*, Arthur Abel quotes Brahms as saying, "I always contemplate my oneness with the creator before commencing to compose. I immediately feel vibrations that fill my whole being. I see clearly what is obscure in my ordinary moods. Straightaway the ideas flow in upon me . . . and, measure by measure, the finished product is revealed." Brahms obviously was seeing *from* the light.

Ah, you say, but the classic composers were geniuses. I will not argue the point. But mediocrity is self-inflicted and genius is self-bestowed. The genius does not differ from others in their access to the light within, only in their confident acceptance of its natural outstreaming.

There is a hidden genius in each person, which each of us gives expression to through commitment, discipline, and the enhusiasm that works with passion. Einstein once said that genius is 1 percent inspiration and 99 percent perspiration. It may be an exaggeration, but it makes a telling point.

You may recall the story told of Paderewski, who had just completed a command performance before some of the crowned heads of Europe. A lady came up to him saying, "Maestro, you are a genius," to which he tartly replied, "Ah yes, madam, but before I was a genius I was a clod." In other words, there is a personal effort required to keep the fire of faith and enthusiasm alive within the mind, and also to make the voice and the hands suitable channels through which the creative flow may unfold or be outformed.

A New Seeing of the World

You may always have thought of the eyes as the windows by which we see the world around us, but perhaps that is not truly how we see. I was fascinated by an article by Jaques Lussyrand that gives a new insight into the process of seeing. It was titled "Blindness—A New Seeing of the World."

The author tells the story of how he lost his eyesight at age eight. He was a brilliant student, and he was increasingly disturbed by the absence of any recognition in education that the world is not just outside us, it is also within. He describes the experience of becoming blind and having the frightening challenge of finding his way between doors and walls and people and trees. But early on he made a discovery—that though he could not see the light of the world outside, the light was still within him. He found that as long as he paid attention to the light within him he rarely had problems getting around. And he also discovered that there was only one way to see this inner light, and that was through love. If he was ever overcome by sorrow, or when anger took hold of him, or if he envied people, his light immediately decreased. He said that sometimes the light went out completely and then he really became blind. But the blindness was not the result of a loss of vision, it was the result of a loss of loving.

This calls for a new insight into love. Love is not an emotion, a commodity that we give and receive, nor can our lives be ruined or empty because we have been deprived of love. Love is neither learned nor taught. We are created in and of love. It is what we are.

We sometimes have mental blocks that impede the free flow of love in and through us. But we are creatures of love. We need to discover what it is in our personalities that turns off the innateness of our being. Lussyrand points out that we are conduits for the flow of Divine Love—and that Love is Infinite.

Light Treatment

This gives a new meaning to Jesus' statement "I am the light of the world." Getting centered in the light within, and then seeing *from* the consciousness *of* light, is actually a "light treatment." When you see from the consciousness of light, you project a flow of light energy that becomes a healing influence. The Hebrew word for "eye" is *ayin,* which means "fountain." There is a natural flowing forth of transcendent light from the eye. In other words, you will no longer see light—you see *with* light. The statement that the eyes are the windows of the soul is apropos here.

"Blessed are the pure in heart, for they shall see God" are familiar words of Jesus' Beatitudes. In an illumined state you see God. This does not mean you see "the man of the skies." But you see *from* the consciousness of God. You see with "God-colored glasses." Your seeing projects the light of Spirit.

At the start of every day the wise student will take a few moments to become established in the light. Hold this realization: "And God said, 'Let there be light.'"

So now, with the frame of reference set, LET THERE BE LIGHT.

· *Exercises* ·

EXERCISE

Light is an eternal reality with no beginning and no end. So "Let there be light" is not the creation of light back there in time. It is the focusing of the light that is ever present in you.

Take a few moments with this breathing exercise: On the inbreath, speak the words

"GOD IS."

Hold it . . .
Then, on the outbreath, affirm

"I AM."

Hold it.

Repeat this several times. Get the sense that you are vitally coupled with the energy of God's light.

With this centering in the light, you see *with* light. And your seeing actually becomes a "light treatment" of all that you see.

Be aware, you did not create the light. Rather, you became synchronized with and in the stream of light that is everywhere present.

Now make a survey of your schedule for the day:

> your appointments..
> contacts
> > projects
> > > and relationships.

As you hold them in the light one by one, you give to each one a "light treatment."

It is only now that you are ready to go into the day because you are giving way to—you are resonating with—the "Let there be Light" of creativity. *Your* participation is what guarantees the "and there is Light."

The whole of Infinite Mind is within you—and you have access to the wisdom of the ages.

EXERCISE

In the stillness visualize a ball of light, such as the sun at sunrise. See that fiery orb coming closer and getting larger. It continues to come closer and get larger until it dominates the entire sky . . . but still it comes, and you go right through it. Now you do not see the light, you see with the light. You are enlightened.

EXERCISE

Visualizing the supportive Universe.

You are seated in a chair in a room in your home. Feel centered in oneness with the Infinite. Remember, you don't have to go anywhere to find God. The wave does not go anywhere to find the ocean—it is the ocean in expression. God is present as a Presence at all times and in all places.

Snap your fingers and your house disappears and you are sitting on the ground.

Snap your fingers and the earth disappears.

Snap your fingers and the sun disappears.

You are now out "in space," surrounded with multitudes of pinpricks of light—above you, beneath you, all around you—all sending their energies to you. Feel yourself centered in this universal energy of support. In the context of this metaphor, how do you pray to God? What is God? God is the Allness of the Universe, focused and centered as you. You are an individualization of the Allness of God. You pray from the consciousness of that Allness, which is rushing, streaming, and pouring into you from all sides while you stand quiet.

Now let's return by the way we came. Snap your fingers and the sun reappears. Snap your fingers and the earth reappears. You are sitting on the ground with no buildings and no people. You snap your fingers and your house reappears with your urban night-dwellers.

Before you let go of this metaphoric visualization, note well: You did not take a space flight "out there." You did not go anywhere. You simply focused on the Reality beyond appearances and experienced your true reality in Oneness. A dynamic prayer power is yours if you remember to pray *from* this consciousness.

Going forward, KNOW:

You are a perfect idea in Infinite Mind. You are whole now. This wholeness is the only way the Universe knows you. When Jesus told us it is the Father's good pleasure to give us the kingdom, he was saying it is the divine nature of the Universe to flow in and through you, fulfilling all you may call your needs.

Feel the security of knowing the Universe is right where you are, supporting and fulfilling you. When your mind is functioning correctly, there is an out-streaming of light from within in the form of inspiration, hunches, leadings, intuitive flashes. Trust this process of inspiration. "In the twinkling of an eye" ideas and plans may flow into your mind. Snap your fingers as a symbolic reminder of how instant and constant the creative process is and how available is your creative genius.

Let the words of the creation—"Let there be light

. . . and there is light"—resonate *as* you, and you will know for yourself: "I am the light of the world, and I let my light shine."

Live in the awareness of the light and you naturally project light in a kind of healing influence. Start your day firmly grounded in the energy of light. And that day will be marked by many

"Magical Moments of Truth."

TWO

Let There Be a Firmament

*And God said "Let there be a firmament in
the midst of the waters . . . and God called
the firmament heaven."*

Primitive man, with no knowledge beyond what could
be seen with the naked eye, considered the firmament the overarching canopy of the sky. Omar

Khayyam, the Persian poet, in his classic collection *The Rubaiyat,* sings of the "inverted bowl of the skies," envisioning it as a giant big-top that covered a flat earth. According to the Hebrew conception of the universe, the earth was surmounted by a rigid vault called the firmament, above which the waters of a heavenly ocean were spread. The early church thought the firmament consisted solely of the sky above, and that the sun, moon, and stars existed for the sole benefit of the earth. Remember that in 1632 Galileo was brought before the inquisition of the Roman Church and made to recant his teaching of the Copernican theory that the earth revolved around the sun. Their focus of perception was outward, on what could be seen. And, since there was no physical proof, their assumption was that the possibility of the sun revolving around the earth could not exist. We have come a long way since then. We now know the "sky" is not a roof over the earth but a perception of a limitless universe around us. What caused this radical change in our perception? Of course, a good deal of scientific study was needed to prove that the universe was limitless. But I like to think that the initial activator that caused scientists to search for this proof was found somewhere inside them, and I like to call this activator faith.

To my mind, faith was the catalyst that led to that recognition. Faith activated the unexpressed possibilities of the mind. Faith created a firmament in the midst of the waters. In the steps of the creation, the recognition of the vastness of the firmament signified a radical change in faith perception.

In the same way, faith is the vital element you need in order to take the second step in the release of your creative genius. And, it is my conviction that in order for your full potential to be unleashed, a radical change in your perception of faith will be necessary—you may need an expanded awareness of what faith *is*.

Unfortunately, it is all too common for faith to

manifest as a parroting of words that express the beliefs of others: "I believe in God," we repeat without really knowing what we mean by that. Too often, all we are expressing is our blind acceptance of a set of beliefs—custom-made convictions—created by others.

In addition to the blind acceptance of ready-made faith, another common problem is lack of faith. Fortunately, there is no such thing. Faith is as natural as breathing. If you feel that your problem is lack of faith, the question you need to ask yourself is what are you believing in. Fear is faith. Worry is faith. Insecurity is faith. The trouble here is not lack of faith, it is simply believing in the wrong things.

If this has been your experience, what you need to work toward is a different perception of faith. Faith is not a commodity, something others may have more of than you. Faith is "the free gift of God"—it is one of your spiritual attributes, which all persons have but only a few use rightly.

One of the great insights of the Bible was uttered by Paul: "Faith is the substance of things hoped for, the evidence of things not seen." In addition, Jesus said, "All things are possible to him who believes." How could he be so sure? Because he had faith that the power of co-creation was indigenous to all persons.

What you need to realize is that releasing your creativity is merely a matter of releasing the power that was "prepared for you from the foundation of the world." For within every person there is a Divine reservoir of inexhaustible wisdom and love and power. It is the sacred deposit in your spiritual genes, which Jesus called "the kingdom of God within you." The apostle Paul referred to it as "the secret that hath been hid for the ages . . . which is Christ in you, your hope of glory." Paul is referring to the divinity that is the true identity of all people. Thus, when Jesus said, "Thy Kingdom come, Thy will be done," the kingdom to which he was referring is the Allness of God which is the Reality of you—your divinity. This is the source of your potential for fulfillment. And the will of which he speaks is the cosmic force that works ceaselessly to reveal it—which you experience as your quest for the creative life.

But before you continue your quest, consider this question: Does faith in God make God work for you, or is it the activity of God in you that is faith? Before you answer, consider this metaphor from the world around you. When the weathervane points to the north, does it make the north wind blow? No. It simply registers the fact that the wind is blowing north. In the same way, faith is not what makes God go to work for you—there is nothing you can do, or think, that will stir God to action.

At first that sentence may feel a bit debilitating, like a door slammed in your face. As a matter of fact, I believe it is not a door closing but a door opening. How can this be? Well, it can be when you expand your thought of God. Once you change your perception of God from a being who has power to the awareness that God is power—the power that does all things, which is already in you—you will realize there is no limitation to your power, only a lack of awareness of it. But before you can alter your awareness, you need to alter your perception; you need to realize that faith is not a vague process of believing in something, it is a positive act of turning on something. When you have made that alteration in your perception you need only to act on the power already within you, a power that is greater than any demand that may be made upon you.

Perhaps you have a rheostat for your dining room chandelier. If so, you know that when you turn it up, you receive more light and power. When you turn it down, light is diminished. There is no miracle involved. The full power is there all the time—you are the one who is controlling the level. A turned-down rheostat might symbolize a faith in lack; a turned-up rheostat, faith in abundance.

The trouble is that, as with so many words in religion, the word *faith* has lost its meaning but not its
use in our language. These days I often find that faith
has become something that is put on on Sunday, like
a Sunday suit or dress, and then, with the final
"Amen," is put back in the six-day closet of unconcern.

We need to take faith back, to reclaim it as our
own and redefine it in a way that is powerful for us.
In his book *The Twelve Powers of Man*, Charles Fil-
more did a study on the spiritual counterpart of the
twelve disciples of Jesus, with each disciple representing one of the foundation faculties of man. In this
study, Peter represents the faculty of faith. How
meaningful that Jesus said to Peter, "I give you the
keys to the kingdom of heaven." This is no namby-
pamby faith; it identifies faith as the key to entering
and working with the dimension of all-possibility, of
accessing your inner genius, your child-of-God self.

Your creative potential is God centered in you.

There is nothing you can do to add to it or take away from it. And your faith in no way alters the fact that God was not more centered in Jesus than in you. However, Jesus was centered in God, while you and I are more likely centered in levels of limitation. In fact, we might consider this a definition of faith— centering your consciousness in God, resonating with the frequency of divine energy. You are not dealing with a God "out there" but a God "in whom you live and move and have being." If this concept is foreign to you, it may also be why the idea of heaven is so difficult to understand. For I do not believe heaven is a place as much as it is a level of awareness, a dimension of life, the vibration of divine energy that is your creative genius.

How can we access this heaven on earth? Physicists have long agreed that everything is energy moving at a different frequency or rate of vibration. A radio station broadcasts at a particular frequency, and anyone tuning in to that frequency will receive the broadcast. Now, as you hold this idea, think again on the quotation from Paul: "Faith is the substance of things hoped for, the evidence of things not seen." Once you tune your mind to the frequency of faith, the evidence of things not yet seen will begin to appear, just as the words and music appear out of thin air from the radio broadcast that you have tuned in to. Substance is the energy out of which all things are created, and it is outformed through our faith.

Consider the watermelon seed. When it is put into the ground, warmed by the sun, and moistened by the rain, it takes off its coat and goes to work. It gathers raw materials from somewhere, equal to 200,000 times its own weight, and by the process of nature a watermelon is formed. Who can look at a slice of watermelon and not be overwhelmed by the colors, the different consistencies, and the fact that out of that one seed has come a fruit with multiple seeds?

Who drew the plan by which the little seed

works? Where did it collect the flavorful extract? How does it develop into a watermelon? It did so because it never questioned its purpose, the viability of its potential. With no knowledge of limitations it was free to become all that God had given it the power to be. We could put many different seeds into the same soil and each will attract what is needed for its fruition. It never varies, it never fails. When a seed is planted in the soil and germinates, there is an implied "Let there be a firmament!" and the creative process is released, each seed bringing forth its own kind.

Can we now accept Jesus' startling statement "All things are possible to them that believe"? Now, this does not mean that you can do things that are not in the flow of your inner potentiality. In a horizontal sense you may fantasize being a star at the Met or with the Mets, but, you see, life flows from within-out in a vertical sense. Let's not confuse the fantasizing of the mind with the vertical flow of inspiration.

What I am talking about here is the energy of your uniqueness—your creative genius, the substance that already exists in Reality. Through your faith perspective you will outform more of your Divine potential than you normally do. When you turn within, centering your attention on God, the center and source of your being, the Allness of you which you may have been expressing only in part, there will come a magical moment of faith's fruition—and that which you perceive inwardly you will soon be seeing in the light of day.

The great teacher said: "If God so clothed the grass, which today is, and tomorrow is cast into the oven, shall he not much more clothe you, O ye of little faith?" What a profound reminder not only of the power of faith but of the innate flow of creativity that is each of us! The Universe that creates a watermelon from a tiny seed, and guides the birds across the uncharted skies, is as focused as you. The same universal process is your creative genius.

The Kingdom of all-potentiality is already within you. You do not need to become something different in order to release it. It calls for knowing that you are (not may be—"Dear Lord, make me be") a spiritual being. Then, armed with this faith perception, you proceed to do what needs to be done. Why? Because faith draws on the infinite, releasing a very real substance that overcomes obstacles, removes mountains of difficulty, doubles one's power, and multiplies one's ability.

There was a time when everyone on earth thought the world was flat. By sailing beyond the horizon, Columbus discovered a new world. Did he make the world round? No, of course not. But he acted on the principle that there was a round world within the flat earth. Thus the New Age insight of holism: There is a round world within the flat one we experience, a whole body within the partial experience of illness, a success reality within the experience of failure.

So be a Columbus and launch out in the direction

of your dreams. The round world will replace the flat one. All that is needed is the commitment to take a stand on the new reality that is the truth of your life.

One thing is certain: To the person with an unshakable faith that something wonderful is going to happen, something wonderful is happening.

So on the second day of creation the Universe said, "Let there be a firmament," and the power of faith was unleashed.

· *Exercises* ·

EXERCISE

Go apart and find a quiet place within. Get yourself centered in Infinite Mind. Visualize an out-
streaming of light synchronized with guidance
and direction.

Affirm, "Let there be a firmament." This is
your faith faculty declaring itself. Feel grateful
in the awareness that you are working with Principle—omnipresent and omniactive. This is
your creative genius in expression.

EXERCISE

Picture a rheostat, recalling that it controls the
flow of electric energy into a light fixture. When

you push the control "up" the light in the room is increased, and when you push it "down" the light is decreased. This is the way mind works in controlling the energy flow in your life. Get still and imagine pushing the rheostat button. Visualize that energy flowing into your mind and body with healing life, prospering substance, and harmonizing love. Practice this exercise often. It is a technique for activating the law of demonstration.

EXERCISE

A radio is a tuner for focusing on a station's frequency and receiving its programming. Each station is assigned a frequency on which to broadcast. If you are forever experiencing certain problems, or if bad luck seems to be hounding your steps, something in you is attuned to the wrong frequency. We may wonder "Why do bad things happen to good people?" But what do we mean by good? A person is not good because he goes to church, or reads the Bible, or lives a religious life. One may be religious and still be extremely negative. If the "sincere religious person" is tuned to WROK, he is going to get the programming of WROK, even if he is sitting in the studio of WGOD. He may be sitting in church seven days a week, but if he is filled with fear or consumed with bitterness, this, and not his religious performance, will determine the experiences he will manifest. If he doesn't like the programming he is receiving, he can tune his receiver to another channel.

As an exercise, contemplate your responsibility of tuning your mind to the right frequency. No matter what you may be experiencing, you always have a choice. Reflect on the reality of a health channel or a guidance channel. In silent meditation, visualize tuning the dial to the appropriate channel. It is a simple illustration, but it can be effective. With repeated practice you will routinely get in tune before every experience.

THREE

•

Let the Dry Land Appear

•

And God said, "Let the waters under the heaven
be gathered together unto one place,
and let the dry land appear."

Because it is easy to forget, I feel the need to reiterate that the Genesis story is not history. Too often
when we read, "In the beginning God created. . . ."

we tend to think of that God in the image of a man, sitting on a billowy cloud saying, "I think I will create a world." But what I want you to see instead is that the creation story is not an event that happened back there in time; instead, it is an articulation of a process that is just as much a part of your life today as it may have been in the antediluvian age.

The trouble is, theologians have always approached religion as a horizontal study, carefully considering the historicity of events, of places and saints and prophets who lived in antiquity. Given that foundation, when we hear the preacher exhort us to "get back to God," we assume he is referring to a literal acceptance of "biblical" times and primitive theology, to a time "back there" when "God walked the earth." What I am asking you to do here is to see the Bible as a creative process, to understand that getting back to God is returning your consciousness to the ground of being, getting yourself recentered in the awareness of your Oneness with God, to see yourself as, in the words of Emerson, "an inlet that may become an outlet to all there is in God."

Unfortunately, because of the horizontal or intellectual perception of Truth put forward by theologians, historical creeds and rituals have been formulated that bear no relevance to our lives today. What I am asking is that you continually remind yourself that when you are dealing with the creative process, you are talking about the working of mind in a vertical or intuitive perception, an infinite potential for unfoldment that works from within you like a fountain.

You and I are thinking creatures, but we think by reason of the fact that we live in Infinite Mind. This is our milieu. You are a point of consciousness within Infinite Mind. You live in the same mind as the greatest seers and prophets of all time. Paul alludes to this when he says, "Let the same mind be in you that was also in Christ Jesus." So you need to realize that revelation is progressive and not a special dispensation of God to someone that occurred long ago—that is a horizontal perception. Once you have faith that revelation is a quality of Divine Mind that already exists in you and everyone around you, you have made the switch to a vertical perception. You are ready to see that what God is revealing to you today may well be more important than what He may have said to prophets and sages of other times.

Psychologists have been telling us for a long time that we are only half awake, that we use but a small part of our mental resources. What you need to realize is that it is not necessary to put something into yourself or catalyze yourself from the outside to achieve that potential. All you need to do is to awaken the process, which is innate, to release your imprisoned splendor. It is important to understand this and have confidence in what I like to call "the process." As discussed in the last chapter, you need faith (that is also innate) that there is an intuitive mind flowing through you, and that your life will become fully functioning only as you confidently work with and trust the process.

Having access to a greater proportion of the All-ness within is often mistakenly referred to as "brain-power." But the brain has no power. It doesn't secrete thoughts as the liver secretes bile. Rather, the brain and the mind are as different as the telephone switch-board and the one placing the call. The brain is the instrument of the mind. The Mind is your infinite God-mind.

The fundamental Truth is that you live in Infinite Mind and your mind is your consciousness within that Mind. You cannot be aware of a need without being in touch with an inner, superconscious re-source. "Before they call, I will answer." Paul says, "For the earnest expectation of the creation, awaiteth the revealing of the sons of God." Cutting through the Bible idiom, this says, "Whatever the puzzling expe-rience, there is an answer in the personal revelation into your wholeness." There is always an answer to the thorniest problem, and that answer is "closer than breathing and nearer than hands and feet," as Tennyson put it.

So, on the third day of creation, when the account reads, "Let the waters under the heavens be gathered together in one place, and let the dry land appear," what you need to understand is that the dry land is the mental image of formed thoughts, the ability to see what *can* be, as opposed to what *is*. *And the power to see what might be is one of the chief traits of the creative genius.*

Unfortunately, the tendency to oversimplify and even debase this process as "holding images" is all too common. We think "I want a new car," form the image of the car we want, and paste the picture on a bathroom mirror where we will see it frequently. This is a problem. When you try to put something that is outside in, instead of releasing that which is inside out, it is a "metaphysical gimmickry," a corruption of a beautiful spiritual process.

The third step in the creative process, then, the creation of dry land from the surrounding waters, deals with imaging from the inside out—what can be called the I AMaging process. And it is not about imaging superficial things and experiences that we perceive with our senses. Instead it is I AMaging, releasing all that we are from within ourselves. This kind of imaging is very creative. It is seeing the dry land while the waters are still gathered together. When this happens, suddenly you may exclaim, "I see!" But what do you see? You are not visually seeing something tangible. You are not seeing an image; you see *from* an image. It is something new, something creative, something that is yours, something that is you.

One of the reasons that many would-be artists do not succeed is that they become inadvertent copyists. They look at the world of superficial appearances and simply reproduce what they see. But a true artist sees with a creative perception that is focused inward, not outward. When you are true to the I AMage, your creative work will be dramatically original.

An interesting example of the power of imaging from within occurred when two psychologists gave forty-five mental patients at a V.A. Hospital some questions and told them to answer the questions as they imagined a well-adjusted person would answer, not as they might spontaneously respond in their self-image of mental confusion. When the responses were tallied, three quarters of the patients showed improvements, some of them quite dramatic. So by acting and even feeling like undisturbed people they proved an axiom articulated by British educator Thomas Troward: "Having seen and felt the end, you have willed the means to the realization of the end."

One of the most impressive misuses of the applications of the imaging power of the mind is worry. Worry is based on the belief that some undesirable condition already exists. You vividly picture it in mind. It becomes an obsession with you. And the way the law works is that because you see and feel the unhappy end, you bring into being its realization.

Worry is one of the most effective illustrations of the warping of prayer. You may say, "I didn't sleep a wink last night. I prayed all night about this problem." But the fact is, you didn't pray at all. You began with "Dear Lord" and closed with "Amen," and in between, you had an orgy of self-pity and paranoia. But true prayer is letting go of the problem and being receptive to the transcendent solution that already exists within you. If you can catch this point, you will save yourself from many sleepless nights.

This is why Jesus said, "Judge not according to appearances, but judge righteous judgment." When you live in the belief that your experience is totally dependent on what happens to you, then every changing condition has the power to pull your strings and determine how you think, or feel, or act. You end up thinking, "Of course I feel hurt. Look what he [or she] did to me." Or if your personal concerns are financial and your attitude is that you are affected by all outer circumstances, then the daily Dow Jones report may be your personal mood meter—and you may react with faith or fear, joy or depression, a terrible way to live. But if you really believe that life is lived from within-out, you will respond from an attitude that Wall Street would describe as bullish. And having seen and felt the end, you will will the realization of that end.

When you begin to realize that you worry by conscious choice, you can choose not to *react* to the outer appearances, but instead to *respond* from the inner flow of ideas, intuition, guidance. Let your faith faculty come forth!

Remember you are an eachness within the Allness of God. You are I AM in expression as you.

It is shocking how many people are bogged down with an "I can't" consciousness, who have "no hope" written all over their faces, who plod along with their jobs, their marriages, their relationships, who conform to all the things that society expects of them, who have given up all hope of change, betterment, help, or healing.

When I speak about this with people, their first line of defense is often "But I don't know how to change!" Of course you don't, because problems cannot be solved with the same energy with which they were created. Here is where the cajoling of the preacher to get back to God makes some sense. For in the awareness of the one presence and power there is not only an answer to the "don't know how," there is a clear direction of how to resolve the how. And it is never in the backward-looking perception of the old theology but in the forward-looking perception of the dry land image.

No philosophy in the world can bring success to the person who is forever indulging his or her emotions with visions of inadequacy and limitation. To be ambitious for prosperity, yet to feel poor, to desire healing and yet always feel weak and afflicted, is like trying to reach east by traveling west. No matter how diligently you work, if you feel less than you desire yourself to be, that feeling is going to neutralize your efforts. The secret of achieving your dreams lies in so vividly imaging them that you literally exude the consciousness of them because you are vibrating with their reality. And the fact will be that you are not creating it from outside yourself, you are resonating with the creative genius within yourself. So if you wish to be prosperous, act prosperously, even dress prosperously; you will draw to yourself prosperous conditions. The Truth is, the possibility of success and achievement exists as a present reality within you right now. But if you imagine you might fail, you will frustrate this inner I AMage, the creative potential, and you will fail.

Industrialist Henry J. Kaiser once said, "It's just as easy to see yourself successful as it is to see yourself as a failure, and far more interesting." You are a visual creature, and thus you are going to imagine yourself in some way, so why not imagine yourself as creative, positive, and good?

The fact is, experimental psychologists have proven that the human nervous system cannot tell the difference between the actual experience and the experience that is imagined. That bears repeating: The human nervous system cannot tell the difference between the actual experience and the experience imagined in detail.

The ramifications of that statement are enormous. For proof, consider the following: An experiment was conducted some years ago at the University of Chicago. A group of students was divided into three control groups. They were taken to a gymnasium, where they took turns shooting basketballs and were scored for proficiency. The first group was told to come back to the gym for one hour a day for thirty days and practice shooting baskets. The second group was told to go home and forget about it. The third group was told to go home and one hour a day for thirty days practice shooting balls in their mind, using their imagination to improve their practice.

At the end of the thirty-day period, all the students were brought back together and each was tested again for accuracy. The ones who had had no practice obviously showed no improvement. The ones who had practiced regularly showed a 24 percent improvement. But the amazing thing was that the people who had practiced only in their mind—I call them "imagineers"—improved by 23 percent. Twenty-three percent to 24 percent—almost identical results. *The nervous system did not know the difference.* Knowing this, look again at what you are imaging. What are you picturing in your mind? Remember, when we talk about imaging we are referring to I AMaging, not seeing the image but seeing *from* the image—the energy of an idea. When you are truly I AMaging you are not copying, you are not reacting; you are releasing your own imprisoned splendor, your own Oneness with the Divine Flow.

Remember Emerson saying: "You are an inlet and may become an outlet to all there is in God"? *All there is*—not just "good enough," not just "making do," not just "I'll make the best of it," but all there is. So let your Allness be revealed. Release your inner beauty, unleash your imprisoned splendor.

Shakespeare describes a process that scientists, inventors, poets, composers, and artists experience when he says: "And as imagination bodies forth the forms of things unknown, the poet's pen turns into shape and gives to airy nothing a local habitation and a name." The scientist calls it "ex nihilo" (out of nothing). In the same sense, your own I AMaging takes hold of what seems to be "airy nothing." (Genesis calls it "the gathering together of the waters") and makes something of it. The dry land appears.

I have often suggested a technique for practicing the imaging process. I call it a "projected diary." At night before you retire write a diary account of the experiences of the day, but with a new twist: Project yourself twenty-four hours hours ahead. Imagine that you are making the diary entry tomorrow night. Then write the account of what happened tomorrow as if it had already happened. This will force your mind to think what you really want to happen. In other words, "Let the dry land emerge." Let the picture unfold from within. This is not to be a forecast of events, nor should it be. But it can be, and probably will be, a predisposition of consciousness that sets subconscious goals.

This will call for a lot of creative thinking, which does not mean sitting around mouthing cheerful platitudes. It means truly tapping into and synchronizing yourself with the creativity that flows from within you.

If this feels difficult, remind yourself that you are a mental creature with the responsibility of controlling what goes on in your mind. As John Milton said, "The mind is its own place, and in itself can make a heaven of hell, a hell of heaven." Your mind exists as a state of consciousness within the mind of God, the same mind that inspired the creative genius of the greatest thinkers of all time. Therefore, you have the power to control the thoughts and images that you hold in your mind. *You always have a choice.* Most of the problems that we experience come from negative mental images that could have been erased at the outset. So don't allow yourself to be someone about whom the poet could say "They die with all their music in them."

It is often said that some project is a "marvel of engineering." The space program and the Internet are examples. But I believe it is more a matter of "imagineering"—well-developed and intelligently guided imagination, creating plans for successful creative action.

Recently I stood before one of New York's miracles of engineering—a skyscraper under construction. In front of this building project was a huge picture of the colossal tower as it will ultimately look. It was a wonderful reminder that great skyscrapers are always impossibilities until the dry land emerges as an image in the mind of the architect.

The trouble is, too many people use the expression "It's only a figment of his imagination." But what would our civilization be like if it were not for the many figments that have led to all the modern developments? Columbus' new world was a figment of his imagination. Edison's incandescent lamp was a figment. Beethoven's Ninth Symphony was a figment. Michelangelo's "Boy David" was a figment. The truth is that your life and mine will reach undreamed-of heights of accomplishment when we take seriously the many figments of imagination that flow through our minds, and cultivate the imagination in a creative and positive manner.

It is imperative to remember: The "let there be" of the creation is evidence of an image in Divine Mind coming forth as the spoken word.

So tap into your creative genius, "let there be dry land," and the dry land will appear.

· *Exercises* ·

EXERCISE

Write your I AMage. If you can type, sit at the typewriter and let your fingers wander idly over the keyboard. Or take a pencil and start to write. Let it unfold, coming out as you. You may amaze yourself with poems, ideas, plans, recipes—all the things you normally think of as coming from exterior sources—coming from within yourself.

EXERCISE

Sit quietly and comfortably. Close your eyes. Take a few deep breaths, and become relaxed in body and mind. Imagine that you are in a sitting position on the edge of a crystal lake. You see the reflection in the lake of the hills in the distance, the trees on the far side of the lake, and the clouds drifting by overhead. Just experience the beauty and freshness of the scene.

Now lean over a little until you see the reflection of your own face; smile, and see your image smile back at you. Reflect on that smiling image, and as you do, see the image change in appearance and become radiant with light. Now see the image take the form of a wise old sage who is looking at you with tenderness and love. Just relax and experience that flow of love and understanding.

Talk to the sage of the lake about whatever is important in your life. Talk especially about your relationships—your relationship with yourself as well as with others—and be aware of the conflicts and problems. Ask the sage in the lake about anything that seems important. Feel the answers come understandingly back, truly "see" the problems of conflicts resolved, and envision the steps that will cause this to happen.

Now go back to the sage in the lake with eyes closed again—and see the appearance change back to your own reflection. Feel good about the fact that the sage in the lake is really you in your transcendent self. Feel grateful that you can communicate with this sage at any time. Know that it is a Presence that is always present. Know that it is a divine flow of love that is always loving you, always a warmth of love in you, always a love force ready to flow forth to love anyone whose life may touch yours.

Gradually, at your own pace, and holding to the awareness of being in the flow of love, become aware once again of the reflections of the clouds and trees and hills in the peaceful lake, and of yourself sitting by it. . . . And let the lake and its surroundings disappear.

EXERCISE

Find a comfortable seated position and clasp your hands together in your lap. Reflect upon the things, situations, persons, and organizations that have some kind of control over you (your spouse, your offspring, styles, your employer, the IRS, mores of society, laws of the land, the finance company, your appetite, what people think about you, etc.). Now think about just one of these controls. Grip your hands tightly in response, remaining aware of your feelings of anger or fear or helplessness. Now think about another one. Grip your hands even tighter. Keep thinking about additional things, each time gripping tighter, until your nails are digging into your palms. Hold this position for a few minutes. Now disidentify—that is, visualize yourself sitting in a chair in front of yourself, looking at yourself going through this exercise of clasping your hands tightly. Say to yourself,

"Why am I holding on to things rather than the other way around? I always have a choice, and I choose to let go. I am free to experience my creative genius!" Now consciously experience a great relief as you loosen your grip and let go. Feel the joyous upsurge of "Aaah!"

FOUR

•

Let There Be Two Great Lights

•

God said, "Let there be lights in the firmament of the heavens to divide the day from the night" . . . and God made the two great lights, the greater light to rule the day, and the lesser light to rule the night.

The sun and the moon: two great lights in the continuum of the creation story. In discussing these lights, I would like to remind you again that the Bible writers were using imagery to tell their tale. Consequently, the first consideration is to discard the image of the sun and the moon as we know them. In the same way, you have (hopefully) ceased to read the creation story as a verbatim reporting of an event in time and space, so you must stop seeing the sun and moon as they were seen by the writers of the Bible. Their accounting renders a picture of a flat earth with a firmament overhead in which the sun and the moon and the stars are hung like props on a stage.

A young child learning to turn lights on would say "Light on" as he flipped the light switch. One night, outdoors with his parents, the child looked up and saw the moon. He cried out, "The moon is on!" It was the wonderful logic of a child. Not just "Oh, look! the moon is there," but "The moon is on." It is an interesting perception—an insight that explains the coming into mind of understanding. It is the focusing of Infinite Mind as you. In the same way your creative energy never disappears, the moon never disappears. Yet both can be hidden, not "on." This happens most frequently when your mind-set becomes locked in a particular orbit or trend.

The fact is a trend is just that. It is not "just the way things are"; rather, it is an indication of your attitude about the way things will be. It is a positive trend (positrend) if you are focusing on that which is good. It is a negative trend (negatrend) if you are hung up on that which is negative. You do not jump from good fortune to misfortune any more than the moon jumps around in its orbit. And even though things sometimes occur as if suddenly and you say "I don't know what happened," things generally don't "just happen." Often they've been happening for a long time. There were trends involved.

Another way to look at the sun and moon mentioned here is to consider how Charles Fillmore, the founder of the Unity movement, regards them. He says that the two great lights referred to here symbolize the awakening of understanding, which is the sun, and the will, which is the moon. Being receptive to your flow of imagination is like basking in the sun. If you remain open, the understanding will come, the knowledge by which your imaginings can be achieved. And with that understanding will come the light of the moon, the will or motivation to go forward. The most important thing to realize here is that the will is the reflection of understanding, just as the moon is the reflection of the sun. However, the will spoken of here is not the will of human determination, but the willingness that gives way to the spiritual process. It is not the will of gritted teeth, but the energy of complete participation with the creative flow.

Remember Moses in the wilderness? He received the guidance to lead his people to freedom from their long bondage in Egypt. Now, note how the creative process worked for him. He encountered a burning bush. It was probably ablaze with the blossoms of spring, but he saw it as "a ball of fire coming to him as an idea." After warming himself next to this light of understanding—this sun—his intuition led him to remove his shoes. In metaphysical symbology, the feet represent understanding, and the shoes represent the intellectual concepts that bind the mind in fixed attitudes or beliefs. When we receive a rich spiritual idea, it is imperative that we "remove our shoes" and become recentered and grounded in the center of light within. The removal of Moses' shoes was a firmament or faith perception that gave rise to the will to lead his people out of slavery in Egypt.

In a mythic saga of personal symbolism, this classic story represents the upward pull of God in every person, a pull that so often goes unrecognized, for despite all our progress as a race there still remains "the enigma of the self." Too often we baffle ourselves with our thoughts and our doings, ignoring that inscription over the temple of Delphi: "Man Know Thyself." And because we do not know who we are we tend to seek relationships and possessions and power and sensual satisfactions . . . not knowing why. St. Augustine wisely observed, "Our heart is ever restless until it find repose in God." But how does a self that we do not understand find repose in God, who may be little more than an intellectual construct—and who is somewhere "out there"?

I feel the answer to this question can also be found in what is generally attributed to St. Augustine: "God is a circle whose center is everywhere and whose circumference is nowhere." This is a fabulous concept, for it not only is a non-definition of God, it is also a powerful articulation of your oneness. For if the center of God is everywhere, then the center of God is where you are. You are at the center. You *are* the center, where you are. Too often, however, we live in the belief that, as the poet Yeats said, "The root of reality is not in the center, but somewhere in the whirling circumference."

Finding the key to effective and creative living is

all about centering, learning to deal with life "con-centrically" (from the center). In a sense it is "the Practice of the Presence of God." But it is practicing concentrically. It is not dealing with God *in* you. It is living and working in the awareness of God express-ing *as* you, opening yourself up to your internal sun, your awareness, as opposed to a hieroglyphic or that which appears outside you.

I recently ran across a reference to Robert Penn Warren, who until his passing was America's beloved poet laureate. And I recalled a little poem of his, the last line of which is (he is speaking of God), "He stared into the dark pit of self, whence all had sprung . . ." And he concludes, "What is man that I should be mindful of him?" These words are remi-niscent of David's Psalm 8, which says, "What is man that thou art mindful of him?" As you can see, the poet turns the image around when he puts his words into the mouth of God: "What is man that I should be mindful of him?" It gives a whimsical turn to a vital

Truth. How can this be whimsical? Because He is God expressing Himself, celebrating Himself, as each of us. Why should He be mindful? Because He has no choice. It is like the body saying, "Why should I be mindful of the hand?" Because the hand is an extension of the body. The body has no choice. In the same way, when you are grounded in yourself, you are also grounded in God. You are an extension of Him, God expressing Himself as you. How, then, could it be possible for your creative genius not to manifest?

In Psalm 8 David goes on to say that man is crowned with glory and honor, and endowed with dominion over all things. At first you may read this as an obvious metaphysical insight, as you may often feel that you are the victim of circumstances. "I am only human," you may say. But David is saying that you are mightier than circumstances. You are not only human, you are human and divine, and the divine in you always transcends the human. You are bigger than your littleness and stronger than your weakness. Living in the light of this understanding, then, you no longer react to the outer, you respond from the inner. You have power and dominion over all life's experiences by the attitude with which you deal with them.

As the creative process unfolds, the dry land appears, a direction, an idea, a project. It is imbued with all the creativity of the Infinite Mind out of which it has come. This is an important facet for you to embrace to awaken your creative genius. The whole of Infinite Mind is present in its entirety in every experience of your life and every idea of your mind. This means that an idea or an image comes replete with the understanding of how to complete it and the will to persevere with the process.

The will is the driving force of life. Thomas Edison was once asked, "What would you have done if you had not finally found the secret of the incandescent lamp?" He replied tartly, "I know one thing. I would be in my laboratory right now instead of wasting my time talking to you." So with Edison, as with all creative minds, the moon is always "on," providing the persistence to keep at it until the plan is completed.

It is this tremendous drive that distinguishes all would-be creators from those who are actively, outwardly creating. For instance, it is probably true that the difference between a writer and a would-be writer is procrastination. Often someone says, "I am going to write a book someday." And he or she really means it. The person has experienced the light of day one, and the faith perception of day two, has felt the dry land image of day three, and the understanding of day four. The light of the sun is shining brightly, but the moon is not "on." The continuum of the creative process is not letting the will be a reflection of understanding as willingness—and this is the focus that is necessary to maintain the driving force of keeping on and keeping on. It is only when this occurs that the *possibility* of the book becomes a reality,

Matthew Arnold, a nineteenth-century English poet, said, "The seeds of god-like power are in us still. Gods are we, bards, saints, heroes, if we will." In fact, you may have the whole making of the book in your consciousness, but if you lack the will you will not proceed.

Many success-conditioning courses attempt to address this problem at the outset. As one course puts it, "Smash the wall that blocks your path to fortune by the projection of your will." This is not an approach I would recommend. As the moon reflects the light of the sun, so the will must reflect the energy of understanding. For when the will acts on its own, it becomes emotional and willful and stubborn, battering down doors to achieve personal goals.

The key here is to understand the subtle difference between will and willingness. When a person says they are trying to find a successful answer to their needs through prayer, they may very well be working by the force of will. An interesting story that illustrates this point concerns one woman who believed that as a child of God she had a right to what she wanted when she wanted it. In this case, she wanted to be married to a particular man. She prayed and affirmed and treated. She said, "He didn't have a chance." Consequently, love didn't have a chance, for they were together for only six months before she began praying to get rid of him. The problem here was that she had reversed the saying: Not my will but thine be done. She thought she knew what was best for her. She did not trust God's plan.

It is my strong feeling that not enough attention is given in the teaching of practical metaphysics to the importance of letting go of the human ego and its willful insistence on demonstrating that it knows best. Affluenza is a pernicious disease that affects many students of Truth. So often there is an attitude of "I know what I want, and I know that in Truth I can have it." So God becomes a genie that hops to our command? This faulty implication is present in much of the teaching of Truth.

The creation story introduces into the lexicon of prayer a phrase that is the prayer that never fails: *Let there be.* Not "There will be," or "Dear Lord make there be," but "Let there be." No suggestion of effort, no strain, no hurry, no anxiety, no willfulness—just let. The Kingdom that Jesus said is within us is a finished kingdom, and that for which we pray is done even before we ask. And when we get the right relationship between the will and understanding, the moon reflects the light of the sun, and becomes an outlet for that which is essentially the Divine Flow. So the will becomes the willingness to let. It is the same urge to go forward, but the emphasis is on "not my will but thine be done." The "let there be" is giving direction to the creative flow.

Granted, this can be hard to remember when life

takes a turn that feels like a closing in or a shutting down: You have lost your job, your lover, your financial security, or a loved one has passed on. When this happens, we tend to react from the human perspective: "Why me?" "Why did this happen?" And so on. These, then, are the times to get centered, to respond from our deep inner self, to take responsibility as co-creator. What trend were we following that caused this to happen? And, now that it has happened, do we have the willingness to acknowledge the trend? The fact is, we always have a choice. The key is this: React or respond.

But what about seemingly incomprehensible events? you ask. The kind that commonly provoke phrases about it being due to "God's will"? Well, this is probably a good time to clear up the confusion about the will of God. Many persons quail at the very mention of the subject, thinking of a divine autocrat who has a capricious intent to make our lives miserable. They think that "His good pleasure" may be at their *expense* rather than their *expanse*, But God's will is the ceaseless longing of the creator to perfect himself in that which He has created. You are a co-creator with God, an extension of the self-livingness of God. God can only will the full expression of your powers and capacities.

This is clearly articulated in the Lord's Prayer: "Thy Kingdom come, thy will be done, on earth as it is in heaven." Here is the powerful secret of prayer that has been obscured in its liturgical use. The fact is the Kingdom is the superconscious mind, present in its entirety as our infinite resource. "Thy will be done on earth as it is in heaven" is the understanding of God's will as His ceaseless longing to perfect Himself in that which He has created, and the willingness to let it unfold in the outer (earth) as it exists in heaven (Divine Mind). In the words of Robert Browning, prayer seeks to "open out a way whence the imprisoned splendor may escape, and not seeking to effect entry for a light supposed to be without."

And when the moon is "on" and the will is properly built into the divine process, then, as Ella Wheeler Wilcox puts it, "that which the upreaching spirit can achieve, the grand and all-creative forces know, they will assist and strengthen as the light lifts up the acorn to the oak tree's height, thou has but to resolve and the whole great universe shall fortify thy soul."

Let the radiant light of spiritual understanding be the fortifying strength of your willingness to reflect the creative process and become the continuum of your creative genius.

· *Exercises* ·

EXERCISE

To practice the principles and the process of this chapter, hold the image of the creation passing before your eyes as a continuum. In the beginning (in principle) God created. . . . Let there be light. . . . Let there be a firmament (faith perception). . . . Let the dry land appear (the image of your projected goal). . . . Let there be two great lights, the greater light (sun / understanding) to rule the day, and the lesser light (moon / willingness) to rule the night. See this as a moving process of the creation (your creative genius) and accept the strength of will to press on to achievement. Practice the continuum each day for a week.

EXERCISE

Reaching for the moon has always been synonymous with doing the impossible, the classic "impossible dream." The man in the moon was always tauntingly remote. But the goal became reachable when we got the moon in the man, by which I mean we got the image of a moon landing in our consciousness. Do you have a desire that appears impossible of achievement? Can you image the fulfillment of the desire, the moon in the man? Let the moon be for you a symbol of doing the impossible. On moonlit nights go outdoors and spend a ten-minute period imaging the moon in the man, seeing your dream made real.

FIVE

Let the Waters Swarm with Living Creatures

*"Let the waters swarm with swarms
of living creatures."*

Ferrar Fenton, a well-known authority in Hebrew and
Greek, says that "God created that which produced
the earth." In other words, in the beginning God cre-

ated the idea of the earth. God-Mind creates ideas, Divine Ideas create thoughts, spiritual thoughts create things. It is a trinity of Mind action that explains the true Creation. In the scriptures "created" means *ideated.* So the creation story is the ideation of the world and all that came forth upon it. It is all taking place in Mind.

The fifth day of the creation represents the process evolving. "Waters" refers to the unexpressed capacities of the mind—your potentialities. The living creatures are the dynamic thoughts in the mind. "Swarming" indicates the supportive activity of Mind, the creative proliferation of multitudes of thoughts and ideas.

"Waters can also be a metaphor for energy." We live, move, and have being in a vast sea of energy. This has been confirmed by the world of science, the world of physics. *Everything is energy moving at different frequencies,* and that energy always gets synchronized with a frequency of like kind. Your thoughts, your ideas are energy. Infinite Mind—everywhere present—is the highest frequency of energy, in which all things exist as complete. When you see the the creative process clearly, your ideas will get synchronized with energy of the same frequency, multiplying in like kind. This is the swarming process.

It is the nature of Mind for an idea to attract swarms of supportive and expansive thoughts. The problem is that we often find this troubling, for just when a dry land image is taking shape and we are beginning to understand how to achieve our goal, our heads race and it appears that our minds are running amok. Suddenly when we most need perfect concentration there is only confusion. At these times it is critical to remember that the swarming of living creatures is part of the process.

To get a clear picture of the secret of the swarm, image a gaggle of geese flying in tight formation, or a school of a million minnows snapping into a tight array, or 10,000 starlings wheeling in close formation over a Kansas cornfield.

At these moments these flocks of birds and schools of fish have a distinctive style of behavior, a fluidity and seeming intelligence that transcend the abilities of the members. The vast flight of starlings is capable of turning en masse, without any one leader. Fish, too, their vision limited in murky water, manage complex, seemingly instantaneous maneuvers when alarmed by an intruder.

The swarm calls for an explanation. It is one of the most interesting phenomena in all of nature, and scientists have long been trying to determine how they are able to accomplish this. The new biology is now beginning to speculate on the possibility that at these moments these creatures lock themselves into a group "soul," letting go of their particular desires and needs as individual creatures and becoming one body with a transcendent intelligence directing them, creating patterns of motion so complex that they seem to have been choreographed from above.

This idea is extremely important to hold on to when we are assaulted with a multitude of swarming ideas. At these times it is critical to be patient and let the swarming take place, to have faith that guidance is a continuum which progressively unfolds to those who believe, and that the chaos of swarming ideas can form itself into a cosmos of organized thought. Jean Jacques Rousseau said, "One must have chaos in him to give birth to a dancing star." In your particular experience of chaos, take time to realize that the same intelligence that made you in the first place continues to guide and direct you. Your chaos is your opportunity to have your own dancing star. For every question there is an answer, for every weakness there is strength, for every lack there is abundance. Let the swarming take place. Out of it will come answers without ceasing.

We have referred to Charles Fillmore's book *The Twelve Powers of Man.* It is a significant study for the student of Truth. Fillmore locates each power at a vital energy center in the body:

The 12 powers are as follows:*

Faith	Discrimination
Power	Understanding
Order	Renunciation
Strength	Love
Imagination	Will
Zeal	Life

(The study relates the foundation faculties to the twelve disciples and the twelve energy centers in the body. It is a fascinating study, but one we will have to leave for another time to explore.)

*From: *The Twelve Powers of Man,* by Charles Fillmore, Unity School of Christianity, Unity Village, Mo., 1933.

Select an idea that could be the spiritual counterpart of a challenge or an opportunity that is facing
you. Using the clustering technique, put the idea in
a box in the center of an 8 ½ × 11 sheet of paper. . . .
Let there be swarming! Let the supportive thoughts
stream forth. Put them in small boxes and position
them around the idea. Let the page be filled with
clusters of thoughts. Then, when the page is filled,
lay it aside for a period of incubation.

The swarming that we observe in nature can also
reveal an insight into the dynamics of group interac-
tion. To be effective, a prayer or discussion group
calls for a kind of bonding that comes from a commitment of love and understanding and the willingness to let go of the ego and give way to a greater
power. Jesus suggests the process when he says,
"Where two or three are gathered in my name, there
am I in the midst of them." While this is sometimes
interpreted to mean that Jesus is in the midst of the
group, it is my belief that Jesus is speaking here in

the absolute, referring to the transcendent awareness of the I AM.

Any assemblage of people, from a great church congregation to a small group gathered for prayer or discussion—as in a business meeting, negotiation session, or research committee—has a "group soul," a cumulative consciousness to which each person gives and from which each one receives. Perhaps we should refer to the prayer group, or the therapy group, or brainstorming group as a "swarming group." The group has its needs and at the same time it contains the answers to its needs. A swarming group can be a powerful instrument for good—a conduit for dynamic ideas.

When ten or twelve people can abandon their ego and humbly let themselves merge into a group consciousness, there will be a natural swarming of the foundation faculties.

You may be seated in a group assembly, such as a church service, and suddenly, "Ahaa!," you sense the answer you have been ardently seeking. Often, in the receiving line after a service, a member of the congregation says, "But how did you know what I needed?" My response, as the Quakers say: "You spoke to my need." The power of the swarm!

To effect this the group session must begin with each person "going down their own well" to make their own contact with the divine flow. Too often, however, the meeting's attendees are plunged into a group prayer before each person has time to touch the secret spring in his or her own heart. Then, after a designated period of individual communion, the facilitator can call everyone's attention to joining together as a group dynamo. This might be symbolized by the joining of hands around the circle. And now by the power of the swarm the group will function as one body. Your problem will become the group's challenge. You will experience an answer because you *are* a spiritual being—not *can* be, but are. It will be *your* answer, though you may think it came from the group. The swarming is not a "brainwashing" for each participant but a "brainstorming," an accessing of supermind energy as it flows from you to you.

For quite some time science has recognized the principle of entropy as a fundamental factor in the universe. Entropy causes organized forms to gradually disintegrate into lower and lower levels of organization. This concept is often linked to seeing the world as a great machine running down and wearing out. It has also had a great influence on diagnostic medicine, which often sees the body living under a death sentence of inevitability of aging, deterioration, and death. Indeed, religious traditionalists have preached that from the day we are born we begin to die, and that God wills sickness for some inscrutable reason of His own.

I disagree with these gloomy notions, and as we enter the new Millennium I think we should take an inventory of the revolutionary insights that are affecting every aspect of life on the planet. For instance, Nobel Prize–winning research biologist Albert Szent-Györgyi posits "an innate drive in living matter to perfect itself." He called for a new fundamental in the universe, coining the word "syntropy." All things from the smallest cell to the universe itself are expanding and being renewed. This means the body is biased on the side of life and wholeness, an idea that is having a profound effect in the field of medicine.

For example, here is an interesting phenomenon that is rarely explained. When a bone break is sustained, there is an immediate severe swelling around the break. Why? The intelligence of the body is creating a natural splint to protect the bone. What better evidence of the law of syntropy and the secret of the swarm. Given this evidence that swarming is an innate intelligence within our body, how can we doubt its healing, rejuvenating effect on our minds?

One way to practice creating order out of the swarms of your mind's ideas is to use a writing technique called "clustering." You start with an idea, then you jot down any peripheral thoughts that come to mind, any one of which may give birth to more peripheral thoughts. You will see emerging a pattern that ties them all together. It is a classic example of swarming. This technique can be applied to any creative process. In every instance, don't seek to shut down the swarm. Rather, open yourself up to it. Then stand back and see how your idea will attract what is needed: the right people, the right conditions, and inspiration from everywhere.

The fact is, we are always dealing with the superconscious mind, which is your mind at the point of God, or of God-Mind at the point of you. There is always an intuitive energy in support of you. We can lay claim to it at any time—and we should. Let day five step of the creation work for you. Let there be swarms of living creatures (supportive ideas). Note that you are not supplicating God for help. You are accessing the help that God seeks to give you: "Let there be swarms. Let!"

The Mind of the Infinite does not do things halfway. It is not possible that a plan will unfold in your mind without there being the knowledge of how it can be completed, the will and persistence to go forward with it, and supportive thoughts with which to work toward the end result. Swarming describes the creative process that is always within as the superconscious mind in which all things are always complete in all ways.

We may logically wonder how we can know which of the swarms of ideas are right for us. That's the beauty of swarming—a vital part of the swarming process is the unfoldment of discrimination and good judgment. If you trust you will know, and know that you know.

Trust the process!

· *Exercises* ·

EXERCISE

Set aside a ten-minute period every day in the park for a week. See how many evidences of swarming you can find: flocks of birds, a swarm of bees, some children forming two teams to play baseball. Reflect on the idea of the "group soul," with each individual creature giving itself up for the greater good of the group. Let it be an evidence of the Presence. And note to yourself how much more the Presence is present with you.

EXERCISE

Use the clustering process to write a story or a report. Begin with an idea of what you want to say. Write it in a box in the center of a blank sheet of paper. Let the mind run freely with swarms of thoughts about the idea. Write a simple explanation of the thoughts in small boxes around the central idea. When the page is full, lay it aside for an incubation period. "Sleep on it." The next morning, meditate on the central idea. You will find yourself attracted to certain of the supportive thoughts, which will unfold in an articulation of your theme. Practice this process with different themes.

•

SIX

Let Us Make Man in Our Image

•

Then God said, "Let us make man in our image, after our likeness. . . ."

From the very beginning of recorded history, humankind has been trying to understand an overwhelming world, one in which we often feel ourselves to be strangers. In an effort to understand this world, we have searched everywhere in the heavens and on earth for answers, searches that have given rise to multiple forms of philosophy and religion. And still the search continues.

As it is possible that not every reader is intimately familiar with the differences between Genesis 1 and Genesis 2, I would like to look at these for a moment before discussing the sixth day of creation, which includes the creation of man. Genesis 1 clearly says that God created man in His image likeness. But then chapter 2 makes the startling assertion that there was no man to till the soil. How can this be? The shocking truth is that in the beginning God did not create the earth, nor did He create man. Rather, Genesis 1 may be more correctly understood as the "ideation" of the world and of perfect man. It is an activity of Mind. Genesis 1 is the *in*volution of creation. Genesis 2 is the *e*volution of creation.

So, the sixth day's phrase is "So God created man

in his own image, in the image of God he created him, male and female he created them"—powerful words, for they express the Oneness of the Universe.

- They encompass the process of the creation beginning with an idea—involution—and then evolving through to fruition—likeness or evolution.

- They establish man as an eternal idea in Infinite Mind with the ultimate destiny to *BE* the likeness of that idea. The phrase "God created man" is a metaphor dealing with the complete spiritual prototype of the creative goal.

- They declare clearly that the male/female energy, representing thought and feeling, is the spiritual nature of the created. And they outline the necessary step of thought and feeling coming together in the process of every creation.

If we then follow that sentence through to its con-clusion—"let us make man in our image, after our likeness, and let him have dominion"—we can clearly see that we have been identified as co-creator, endowed with the innate knowledge of the creative process. (creative genius). We can also see a clear statement of the dominion of the spiritual being. It is important to note that in speaking of dominion here, I am not defining it as power, as so many people do. Rather, I am speaking of dominion as the creative dominion of the superconscious, the Reality of each person. If you look at Webster's dictionary you will find that in addition to being defined as as domain, dominion is also defined as supreme authority and absolute ownership. This is your birthright, then, the absolute ownership of your creativity.

The image in which you are created is your true Self Image, which only you can express. Remember, there are no duplicates in the creation; every snowflake, every blade of grass, every grain of sand—a unique design. In the same way, there has never been anyone—nor will there ever be anyone—just like you. You are a unique expression of the creative energy of the Universe focused eternally as you. Yes, you are a Divine Original! And the divine intent active as you has one desire: to express expansively and creatively its uniqueness as the perfect idea it is in Infinite Mind. This is your spiritual destiny. Having this understanding, that the creative process never duplicates itself, eliminates all covetousness and competition.

Traditional Christianity talks of Christ as the "only begotten son" and contends that all the rest of us are only "miserable sinners," completely dependent for salvation on accepting the "only begotten." I think that this is misleading and that part of the confusion comes when the names Christ and Jesus are used interchangeably. I believe Jesus discovered the divine dimension in Himself (the Christ Self). This was the key to Jesus' acceptance of his divinity, and he made it clear that this same divine dimension is the root reality of each one of us. He said, "All that I do you can do also." The most individually identifying statement in the Bible is "Christ in you, your hope of glory." Christian tradition has long erroneously maintained that Jesus in you is your hope of glory. But the Christ is not Jesus. It is the divine reality of Jesus that he discovered in himself and that is also in you. I call it your Super Self.

But what should we make of the phrase "only begotten son"? Meister Eckhart, that amazing medieval mystic monk, has an answer to the question: "God never begot but one son, but the eternal is forever begetting the only begotten." This says there is only one pattern or prototype for man, and that is the Christ, and that Christ is incarnated in each of us. It is the spiritual reality that is each person's true identity.

In the development of the person there are many influences that help to shape their character and consciousness. Consequently, it may be said that they are begotten of family traditions, of passing fads, and of the values of "one's time," but the truth is they are begotten only of God. In the same way that the Christ—the Reality of Jesus—was begotten of God— the Christ—the Reality of you—is begotten of God. It is the expression of this Reality that we call your creative genius.

As I stated in Chapter 4, "God is a circle whose center is everywhere and whose circumference is nowhere." So, then, the center of God is where you are. And the manifestation of this center is the begetting of God in you, you as God. Unfortunately, the world we live in today is often a maelstrom of things and ideas, and when we get caught up in this maelstrom we forget the Truth of God in us. Consequently, we need to develop a personal technique of centering. Jesus described it in utter simplicity: "Enter into the inner chamber and close the door, and pray to your Father in secret." This is the "still point" within us where Infinite Mind is individually focused as your superconscious mind. By observing regular periods of meditation we can learn to harness our superpowers to get centered in the oneness of our Super-Self. Now, some of you may be turned off by the reference to meditation. You may think meditation has nothing to do with the Christian tradition, that it is an Eastern phenomenon. Or you may feel it necessitates sitting cross-legged on a chaise, contemplating your navel. But meditation is nothing more than getting centered in your reality, where you can freely access the mind of God. It can take many forms of expression, some of which I will discuss in the exercise section at the end of this chapter.

Having found a method of meditation that works for you, you will no doubt begin to grapple with many questions. One of the most crucial questions faced by Truth-seekers through the ages is that of duality: the belief that there is in each of us a human person and a divine person. This idea has been fostered by traditional religion, which has emphasized the purely human—judging the person as a miserable sinner, with frustrations and evil inhibitions ever seeking to wreak havoc in our lives. Psychology has followed in the same analysis of the human—using terms such as "sex drive" instead of the devil, but coming to much the same conclusions. This sense of duality was addressed clearly in the Old Testament: "God created us upright but we have sought out many inventions" (Eccl. 7:29 ASV).

It is heartening to report, however, that there is an awakening taking place in both psychology and religion. For example, depth psychologist Ira Progoff says that neurosis occurs because something creative and meaningful is seeking unsuccessfully to express itself in the life of the individual, and that a person is not a bundle of repressions but a bundle of possibilities. Progoff feels the key to therapy lies in the reactivation of the process of growth. This frees the creative idea to manifest in its purest form as your Super-Self.

Wherever you may be along the way of your unfoldment, the whole of you is always present even within your partial expression of it. I like to say, "There is an Allness within your illness, an all-sufficiency within your insufficiency." This is the Super-Self, that which is created metaphorically in the creation story. And the Super-Self is not a different personality. It is the radiant self of you, the whole person you are and have always been.

New Thought teachers and students delight in talking about a "great sleeping giant" of your divine reality, a kind of genie to bring out of a bottle for use in working out personal problems. But this is a duality that can lead to great confusion. The Universe is whole, and you are that wholeness in the process of being you. God can never be less than God, and your Super-Self can never be less than your divine image.

Your potential is not something you might *possibly* achieve. It is a reality even before you discover it. It is that of you that is always whole, even if the surface self is ill or confused or lonely.

You might want to accept and declare for yourself the following powerful statement: "Within me is the unborn possibility of limitless living, and mine is the privilege of giving birth to it."

The trouble is that too many of us are trapped in a "time/space consciousness," relegating spiritual growth to an "afterlife." Do not allow this to happen to you! You *are* created in God's image-likeness— not *were* or *may be.* It is not something you once had and perhaps lost, or something you might *possibly* achieve. It is the reality of you right now; you are now endowed with the full power and Reality of Spirit. This is the promise of the sixth day of creation. It is a Reality in Mind. It already exists. This Reality is the source of your potential, and you will have to evolve that which has been involved in you.

"God created man in his image-likeness" refers to the prototype or potential of the evolutionary man. Paul had this in mind when he said, "Christ in you your hope of glory." Christ is the true nature of Jesus, his indwelling Reality—and ours. The seven steps (days) describe the process of the unfoldment of that Reality, which is clearly seen in the life of Jesus, who said, "All that I do you can do too, and greater things than these shall ye do."

This can be proved. Throughout history, there have been people who have released the inner awareness of their divinity. Plotinus, a third-century A.D. Egyptian neo-Platonic philosopher, had a unique awareness of the sacred secret of transcendent life. He envisioned a creative flow of life and intelligence from within—that the key to abundant living is to keep centered, and that the whole universe rushes and streams and pours into us from all sides, while we sit quiet.

Reading this, the logical mind will notice a contradiction. How can Plotinus envision a creative flow of life and intelligence from within, and say that the whole Universe rushes and streams and pours into us from all sides? The answer is in the word transcendence, or Oneness. It is not time-space consciousness—it is simply consciousness. When you go within in meditation, you do not actually go anywhere. In stillness you center your attention upon the highest vibration, "the contemplation of the facts of life from the highest point of view," and this opens up a world within that is in complete harmony with the world without. You no longer see a duality. From this consciousness you can then listen to an inner "voice" that you will hear without ears, and experience inner visions that you will see without eyes. And once you open yourself up to this reality it can be the theme of many wonderful meditations with which you begin the day. Having done this, you will then go forth into your world fully prepared to meet and conquer any contingency, for your meditation will have shown you that there is no duality between you and your world. There is simply the Oneness in which you exist and out of which you create.

Please note that this meditation is not an attempt to change anything. Your goal is not to set things right, but to see them rightly. There is an old hymn that says, "Everywhere change I see. O Thou who changest not, abide with me." Too often, like the Prodigal Son, we go off into the far country wishing and wanting. And like the Prodigal Son we need to "come to ourself" and become centered in our Self in which there is only wholeness.

I have spoken of Moses before, but I feel it is important to come back to him. When the plan dawned in Moses' mind to lead his people out of slavery in Egypt, he demurred, saying, "But I am slow of speech. How can I convince them?" Having said this, he had an inner realization: "Go and I will be thy mouth, and I will teach thee what thou shall speak." And when Moses asked, "But who shall I say sent me?" God said unto Moses: "I AM that I AM. . . . This is my name forever and this is my memorial unto all generations" (KJV). This is the Presence—the image of each person's creation—declaring Itself. Moses had to go inside to become aware of his true identity, conscious of the I AM power. Only then, with the awakening of the will to achieve, could Moses go forward to accomplish his mission. He had to turn inward before he could effectively turn outward.

Bible translators have always been confused by this use of I AM. In Genesis 4:26, the translation most of us have read says, "Then began men to call upon the name of the Lord." However, in the King James Version this is rendered, "Then they began to call themselves by the name of the Lord." These words express their awakening to their true identity—which means something entirely different. Unfortunately, later translators could not understand this, so they changed it. (Some versions of the Bible have a marginal reference explaining it was changed "for clarity.") But this changes the whole meaning of the "I AM," and this is the key to affirmative prayer. "I AM a perfect child of God" means God is perfect and I am perfect, created in His image-likeness. The Super-Self of me reflects this perfection.

The reason it is so important to call ourselves by the name of the Lord, to claim our own oneness within the divine process, is that in our quest for creative genius we stumble if we see the creation story as finding better ways to call upon God for "heavenly handouts." The Allness of the creation is present in its entirety within each of us. If we do not embrace this, we are left with the idea that Jesus was God's only son, and that all we can do is accept Jesus as our intermediary with God, the giver of the heavenly handouts. But remember he said, in effect, "Don't look to me, but find the Christ in you as I have found it in me."

An example of the divine flow innate within us

can be found in the story of a youngster watering the garden with a soft plastic hose. When the water stopped flowing freely, he called to his father, who was nearby: "Daddy, something's wrong with this old hose. It won't work." The father saw the trouble at a glance. "There's nothing wrong with the hose, son," he said. "It's just that you are blocking the flow. Take your foot of the hose and see how well the water will come through for you." How many of us are standing on the hose and blocking the flow of creativity in our lives? Too many. But the fact remains that the person who says their creativity has "dried up" is standing on their hose. Their confidence has waned. Their self-worth has lowered. Their attention has become divided. But creative ideas are ever present as the possibility of fulfillment.

Too few of us remember that creativity is an integrative process, that we need to take time to consciously establish our oneness—to get into the flow. We need to let our hands and heart be channels for the flow of wisdom and creative ideas. As the poet Adelaide Anne Procter suggests in her classic poem "The Lost Chord," let your fingers wander idly over the keyboard (or the computer, the workbench, the sewing machine, or the cookstove). And you will touch your own "lost chord," which will "quiet pain and sorrow like love overcoming strife." And it will be to you the "harmonious echo from your discordant life. . . . It will link all perplexed meanings into one perfect peace."

· *Exercises* ·

EXERCISE

In that still place within where only you can go, let the energy of the words "let us create man in our image and likeness, male and female created he them" move through you. Be as an observer. You are witnessing your creation. Feel yourself unlimited by space-time. Understand and accept your eternal essence.

EXERCISE

Focus on an idea, an inspiration, a deep desire that you may be working on. Accept the spiritual dominion that is yours—move through the steps of the creation. Participate as co-creator and let the image come forth in its likeness. This is your creative genius.

EXERCISE

Take an inventory of negative or limiting declarations you have claimed for yourself. You know your own list. Recognize this is the conscious mind (the intellect) that judges by appearances and is not in tune with the creative flow. Now turn them around using the words "I AM." Identify yourself by the name of the Lord, I AM:

> "I AM Life, vibrating as perfect health in every cell, organ and function of my body."
> "I AM the radiant Light of pure knowing."
> "I AM established in the divine flow of substance."
> "I AM protected. I live 'under the shadow of the almighty.' "

"I AM Love, and I AM secure in the the energy
of all true relationships."

This is your creative genius, which knows
its oneness in the Source (Infinite Mind, or
God), and the words are powerful—they are the
spoken word of creation. Jesus understood this
when he said, "These are not my words but the
words of Him who sent me."

EXERCISE

Practice accessing the everywhere-present
Mind of God. This is a powerful form of meditation—an experience of Oneness. (You might
want to think of the Internet, where you can immediately access any kind of information available anywhere, anytime). When facing a need
for guidance, or for success in business, or for
harmony in relationships, get still, let go of all
sense of reaching out there, center your atten-

tion on the still point, and be receptive. Feel secure in the awareness that the correct answer exists in Divine Mind. Remember that you are an inlet and may become an outlet to the whole of Infinite Mind. Let there be the coming together of thought and gratitude, of image and likeness, of idea and fulfillment.

SEVEN

·

God Rested

·

And on the seventh day God finished his work
which he had done . . . and he rested . . .

Day seven of the creation story is a classic example
of anthropomorphism. It seems to suggest that God
has just been through an exhausting experience of
personal creation, and so He rested. But if you hold
that perception, then the creation that was accomplished 6,000 years ago was something God did. Re-

member, however, that this is actually the involutionary creation. It is Divine Mind acting upon itself,
formulating an idea of the creation. It is finished in
Mind, even though there is still "no man to till the
ground." To reiterate, the real miracle was the immi-
nence of the creative process in the field of Infinite
Mind. God did not *try* to make a world. It was Mind
creating out of itself, simply saying "let there be" to
every step of the creation. And it is when we understand the power of "let" that we discover how we can
release the energy of our own creativity. In the seeming inactivity of "resting" there is the cumulative activity of the six steps coming to fruition.

Each of us is on a lifelong quest for truth: for
meaning, for self-realization, for creative expression,
for the awareness of oneness with God. But the truth
we refer to is often not a set of definitions or a creed
that we can settle on in a "confession of faith."
Rather, it is a pathway along which we travel, a way

of life that requires practice and discipline and persistence.

A traveler in ancient Greece had lost his way and, seeking to find it, asked directions of a man by the roadside who turned out to be Socrates. He asked, "How can I reach Mt. Olympus?" To this Socrates is said to have gravely replied, "Just make every step you take go in that direction."

You see, there is only one way under the sun by which man can achieve his Mt. Olympus—that is to say, achieve the realization and unfoldment of his own creativity and salvation in the truest sense of the word—and that is by bringing about a radical and permanent change for the better in his own consciousness. But this is rarely something that happens overnight. More often it is a process of "letting" and resting. For the true Mt. Olympus is not the summit of the hill, it is the pathway up the hill. As I often say of success, it is not getting there—it is earning the right to be there. And the earning is a constant process of practice, practice, practice.

It is interesting to note that religion as we know it had its inception in what I call "creative intermission," or Sabbath. The fourth commandment says, "Six days shalt you labor—but the seventh day is a sabbath to the Lord your God." The word *Sabbath* means "rest." The religions of Judaism and Christianity have evolved from primitive roots that were sabbatarian, meaning the practice was centered around a sabbath day. In fact, the early Hebrews were a theocratic society with religious laws that carried the death penalty for breaking them.

An example of this can be found in the story (Numbers 15:32) of the man found gathering sticks on the Sabbath. He was brought before the elders, who condemned him to death by stoning. "And all the congregation stoned him with stones, and he died . . . as the Lord commanded." An interesting commentary on the prevailing God concept! Consider, too, that the religious traditions in America have evolved from many influences of our Puritan forebears: The Sabbath Day is the centerpiece. And while people are no longer stoned for breaking the Sabbath, it has been made a sin not to go to mass or church. Churchgoing has become a badge of conventional respectability.

And within the religious communities that espouse this idea the erosion of moral and spiritual values in the marketplace, the "secular society," is seen as the work of the devil. But it is my feeling that it is institutional religion that has helped to make this secular society by creating these artificial divisions of sacred and secular, of holy days and weekdays. In these institutions the church is usually a place set apart, conducted by a clergy, who are a class set apart, on the Sabbath, which is a day set apart. Given this, is it any wonder that many of their congregants tend to go through a "performance" on Sunday, and then on Monday put their religion back into the six-day closet of unconcern? The key to day seven of the creation is the mindful observance of daily Sabbaths or creative intermissions. And these creative intermissions should not be dictated by outside forces or external surroundings. When you get still, get centered in God-in-you, then there is a natural rhythmic flow of the universe; work and rest, outpouring and infilling. This stillness allows you to know that God cannot be more present anywhere than he is present everywhere. God can only be found within ourselves. We do not need to go to a church to find Him. And when we are in a sanctuary of prayer, God is present (for us) because we are present.

The native Hawaiians have an unusual word for visitors to the islands: *haolis*. Why? When the Christian missionaries first arrived they set about to convert the natives from their pagan ways, setting up little chapels in which the people should worship God. But when the native Hawaiians went there, they found one thing quite strange. Whereas in their

Kahuna practice they always followed their times of the worship of their gods with a period of silence to "breathe life into their devotions," the Christians simply rattled off their prayers, got up, and walked out. This led the natives to call the Christians, and later all visitors to the islands, *haolis;* the word means "without breath." And this breath, this rest, is the true spirit of the seventh day of creation. The Sabbath day is the time, *any time,* when you remember the Allness of good that is present right where you are, when you take time to let Spirit breathe life into your whole being, to pause and become centered in the divine flow of life, love, and substance.

A wonderful example of this anytime anywhere Sabbath can be found in the story of a highly successful businessman who has a prayer time in his office every morning at ten o'clock. This has been a daily ritual with him for twenty-five years. His secretary takes no calls and all business must wait while he has his ten-minute Sabbath. Yet the man never goes to church. In fact, he regularly plays golf on Sunday, causing his "religious" friends to call him a sinner and pray for his salvation. However, this man's church is an inner experience that he faithfully observes every day.

Some years ago, *Time* magazine featured a cover that boldly read, "God Is Dead." This caused a great shock wave to travel through the traditional establishment—blasphemy, sacrilege! Actually, this dissent by radical theology was a healthy period in religion. It reflected humankind's growing unwillingness to accept custom-made convictions, and their inability to find help or inspiration from an ancient definition of God. Perhaps it was Emerson, one hundred years earlier, who inspired this radical dissent when he said, "When we have broken with our God of tradition, and ceased from our God of rhetoric, then may God fire us with his presence." It was the call to mysticism.

This is not to denigrate the church. There is something very special about a group of people who let go of self and its ego needs, and give one's self over to the larger good of the group. The world needs what the churches *can* give, and every person may be immeasurably blessed by being a part of that giving. However, churches could be much more effective and Sunday attendance much greater if the emphasis were more on teaching than on preaching, on helping people to find their spiritual center rather than on demanding loyalty to a place of stone and stained glass.

Henry Drummond, the Scottish preacher, angered many of his confreres in the ministry when he said that the main purpose of the church was to help people to get along without it. What they did not understand was that he was not advocating the breakup of the Church but rather the breaking down of its creeds into a practical way of life. He was saying that the Church should see itself as a school or college whose role is to make the student self-reliant and to make itself progressively unnecessary. He felt that a good

Christian or Jew was not just a Sabbath day communicant but one who experienced his communion with God often, wherever he might be, by entering the quiet sanctuary of the soul.

To remember the Sabbath day is to periodically check up on yourself to determine if you are living, loving, and working in the flow of universal rhythm. You might reflect on the ebb and flow of the tide, the rising and setting of the sun, the changing of the seasons, the diastole and systole of your heart. Did you know that there is a contraction and dilation of the heart seventy-five times a minute, week after week, month after month, year after year?

But given that, you may wonder how the heart can be included in a list of things that come and go. The answer is in day seven of the creation: "God rested." You see, the heart is not constantly at work. Following every contraction there is a vital period of rest. Studies have revealed that out of every twenty-four hours the heart is still for a total of fifteen hours. Isn't that amazing? In fifty years of beating the heart has actually been at rest for thirty years. A dramatic demonstration of the creative intermission!

Have you ever noticed that on finishing a task, especially one that has been prolonged and required much skill, effort, and perseverance, we heave a sigh? It is a symbol of relief and release from tension. It is a kind of sabbath. If we can take the time to be aware of and acknowledge this, we will realize that just beyond this comes an inbreathing that could symbolize an inflow of Spirit. We would do well to keep this in mind, to identify the sigh of completion as a "Sabbath unto the Lord," a thanksgiving, with the next breath as a new opportunity to "let there be." It is but one step beyond this to the disciplined practice of the Presence through the day.

There is an old hymn, "Take Time to Be Holy." Good advice! Take time to be established in the awareness of wholeness, Oneness in the Divine Flow. The benefits are great. You will find increased ability to make decisions and to unfold creative ideas. You will easily rise to the challenge of even the most difficult human relations. It will improve both your disposition and your health. In the marketplace of life, peace may seem elusive and even unattainable, but it comes easily to the mind that is disciplined to the creative intermission.

This is particularly important given the exciting times in which we live. Witness the very rapid expansion in our technology, in the medical field, in science and physics. What were once dreams, desires, even fantasies have become living ideas that are accepted first as possibilities and move quickly into the world of manifestation or reality.

Moving into the third millennium, we will all be expected, and indeed we will expect of ourselves, to participate as co-creators in an expanding Universe. Emerson said, "There is guidance for each of us, and by lowly listening we will hear the right word." It is my hope that this book on creative living may have suggested to you the "right word," and revealed to you the "Sacred Secret" of your capacity to give birth to a very special and unique unfoldment of God expressing as you—your creativity! Now that you have come to this realization, you can begin to direct your God-given creativity into channels of Truth and beauty, and use it in the fine art of living. In the secret hidden within us is the potential to experience boundless energy, to receive the ceaseless flow of creative ideas, to attract limitless abundance, and to outform in our bodies in radiant life and health.

As Ralph Waldo Trine says in his *In Tune with the Infinite*, "The great central fact of human experience is the coming into the conscious, vital realization of our oneness with this infinite life, and the opening of ourselves fully to this divine inflow."

The reality of God is eternal energy, present in its entirety at every point in space. Energy was never created, it was only harnessed, taking the form of love, of faith, of wisdom, of substance. So the whole creation is involved in Infinite Mind, and our role as co-creators is to evolve in the manifest realm that which has been involved in Mind.

During the early days of World War II, King George of England, in a radio message to the world, quoted these lines from M. Louise Haskins: "I said to a man who stood at the gate of the year, 'Give me a light that I may tread safely into the unknown.' And he said unto me, 'Go out into the darkness and put your hand into the hand of God. It shall be unto you better than light and safer than a known way.' " Are you ready to let go of the "safety of the known way" of the intellect and be receptive to the unique expression of your creative genius?

Hold this realization in consciousness: "I establish myself in the awareness of the sacred secret of the Christ indwelling, the hidden genius of my God-self in my thoughts, words, and actions. I give it full exposure, that all the world might see and rejoice with me that I AM WHOLE."

· *Exercises* ·

EXERCISE

In a frank and honest self-inventory, ask yourself the question "What are the major disap-
pointments of my life in terms of work,
investments that did not pan out, creative projects that never matured?" Make a list of them
in your notebook. Now ask the challenging
question "Why?" "Why hasn't the creative flow
worked for me?" Reflect on this puzzling
dilemma for a few minutes. Let your mind come
up with answers. Be objective, not critical. Realize that the answers may be little more than al-
ibis or excuses or rationalizations or attempts at

self-defense. They may indicate a sense of un-worthiness. Know that if they come to you they are in *your* mind, and if they are negative, they may well be blocks to the free flow of abun-dance. We might call them *icons*, for indeed we worship them as idols. Here are a few examples:

"I have been unlucky."

"My employer does not appreciate me."

"I was not able to go to college because I had to support my family."

"I was always told I would not amount to much."

"I am too young to retire but too old to get another job."

Now close your eyes and visualize a room with many little alcoves in the walls. Consider your "answers" and see how securely you have installed each into an alcove as an icon. Stand back and look objectively at what you have been creating: a "Pantheon of Icons of Limitations."

You are not judging or blaming; you are seeing with a new insight. Now, taking responsibility as co-creator, exercising your power of choice, see a figure with a coat of many colors (creative imagination) come into the hall, walk around the room, and firmly declare: "I do not relate to any of this." Then see the figure take action, placing all the negative icons in a wheelbarrow, wheeling them outside to a receiving dock, and dumping them into a waiting refuse truck. As the truck drives off, the figure with the coat of many colors triumphantly announces, "I am free at last!" Hear sounds from the receiving dock of your consciousness. It is the arrival of a new shipment of icons, which are addressed to the newly named "Pantheon of Icons of Creative Abundance."

EXERCISE

The art of decision making. You stand at a crossroads. It is important to realize that you cannot make a wrong choice. The right choice is known in you—and it is known by you at the superconscious level. This is not to suggest predestination. The only predestiny in life is the ultimate unfoldment of the divine creature that you are. But the direction you take is determined by your consciousness.

What is it you need to know? Write it down so that you are clear about it. Rest for a moment in your awareness of oneness within Infinite Mind—no strain, no worry, no fear. Just quietly reflect on the Truth that within you, you know. Then lay the decision aside for a time of "creative intermission." Give yourself a deadline. (I prefer to call it an "alive-line.") Know you have made a divine appointment with an idea. Do not talk about it. Do not ask people for advice. Let the process work through you, as it surely will. Then, at the predetermined time, act as if the decision is already made—which it really is, within you. Launch out, move your feet. You will find yourself easily taking the action that is correct—one step leading to the next—without ever having to formulate the decision for yourself. Trust the process. You will not have to make the decision—the decision will make you. And be prepared for some "divine surprises."

This is an exercise that you can work with as an ongoing habit.

Epilogue

We have seen that the story of creation is not a record of the accomplishment of an anthropomorphic God. It is an allegory, a hieroglyph that contains a personally created symbolic message for the seeker of light.

So . . . Genesis is involutionary, a forming of creation in Mind. But why did the process of creation commence? In the absolute and profound silence, what was the step in creation before, "Let there be light"? Was it the creative pause—the focus within—vibrating as the primal, eternal, divine manifestation? I believe it was the desire to give love form, physical substance. Because God is Love and the creation is love in action, the absolute, the profound, could no longer remain silent. The "Let there be light" was as a spiritual combustion—Love creating out of itself.

In the 1950s British Cosmologist Fred Hoyle coined the word "big bang," referring to the theory of the creation which has helped scientists work out a mechanistic, gears-and-levers theory of the Genesis moment itself—the hows, if not the whys, of creation ex nihilo.

In the stream of creative imagineering, could it be that the dynamic energy of the Universe chose to take form—the idea coming together in and with love resulted in the "big bang" and creation started? And, as co-creators, could it be that each time a creative idea comes together in and with love, there is a micro big bang and the creation continues? While it is difficult for the human intellect to comprehend the profoundness of Infinite Love, the important thing to hold on to is that we are created in its image-likeness. It is this concept that we must draw on to source the manifestation of our own creativity—our own love which sources itself from God's love, and it is this concept that makes all the products of our creativity complete and good.

As we look at our past, it is exciting to see the evolution of human knowledge. As we look to the future, science and technology—symbolized by the Internet—are blazing a breathtaking highway into the future. If we, ever so often, wonder, "What is happening?" we can know the answer, "God is happening" . . . "life is happening" . . . "I am happening" . . . "love is happening." May you enjoy the fruits of your creative genius!

Creation

In the beginning God created the heaven and the earth.

And the earth was without form, and void; and darkness was upon the face of the deep. And the Spirit of God moved upon the face of the waters.

And God said, Let there be light; and there was light.

And God saw the light, that it was good; and God divided the light from the darkness.

And God called the light Day, and the darkness he

called Night. And the evening and the morning were the first day.

And God said, Let there be a firmament in the midst of the waters, and let it divide the waters from the waters.

And God made the firmament, and divided the waters which were under the firmament from the waters which were above the firmament: and it was so.

And God called the firmament Heaven. And the evening and the morning were the second day.

And God said, Let the waters under the heaven be gathered together unto one place, and let the dry land appear: and it was so.

And God called the dry land Earth; and the gathering together of the waters called he Seas: and God saw that it was good.

And God said, Let the earth bring forth grass, the

herb yielding seed, and the fruit tree yielding fruit after his kind, whose seed is in itself, upon the earth: and it was so.

And the earth brought forth grass, and herb yielding seed after his kind, and the tree yielding fruit, whose seed was in itself, after his kind: and God saw that it was good.

And the evening and the morning were the third day.

And God said, Let there be lights in the firmament of the heaven to divide the day from the night; and let them be for signs, and for seasons, and for days, and years:

And let them be for lights in the firmament of the heaven to give light upon the earth: and it was so.

And God made two great lights; the greater light to rule the day, and the lesser light to rule the night: he made the stars also.

And God set them in the firmament of the heaven to give light upon the earth.

And to rule over the day and over the night, and to divide the light from the darkness: and God saw that it was good.

And the evening and the morning were the fourth day.

And God said, Let the waters bring forth abundantly the moving creature that hath life, and fowl that may fly above the earth in the open firmament of heaven.

And God created great whales, and every living creature that moveth, which the waters brought forth abundantly, after their kind, and every winged fowl after his kind: and God saw that it was good.

And God blessed them, saying, Be fruitful, and multiply, and fill the waters in the seas, and let fowl multiply in the earth.

And the evening and the morning were the fifth day.

And God said, Let the earth bring forth the living creature after his kind, cattle, and creeping thing, and beast of the earth after his kind: and it was so.

And God made the beast of the earth after his kind, and cattle after their kind, and every thing that creepeth upon the earth after his kind: and God saw that it was good.

And God said, Let us make man in our image, after our likeness; and let them have dominion over the fish of the sea, and over the fowl of the air, and over the cattle, and over all the earth, and over every creeping thing that creepeth upon the earth.

So God created man in his own image, in the image of God created he him; male and female created he them.

And God blessed them, and God said unto them, Be

fruitful, and multiply, and replenish the earth, and subdue it: and have dominion over the fish of the sea, and over the fowl of the air, and over every living thing that moveth upon the earth.

And God said, Behold, I have given you every herb bearing seed, which is upon the face of all the earth, and every tree, in the which is the fruit of a tree yielding seed; to you it shall be for meat.

And to every beast of the earth, and to every fowl of the air, and to every thing that creepeth upon the earth, wherein there is life, I have given every green herb for meat: and it was so.

And God saw every thing that he had made, and, behold, it was very good. And the evening and the morning were the sixth day.

Thus the heavens and the earth were finished, and all the host of them.

And on the seventh day God ended his work which he had made; and he rested on the seventh day from all his work which he had made.

And God blessed the seventh day, and sanctified it: because that in it he had rested from all his work which God created and made.

Genesis 1:1–2:3 (KJV)

ABOUT THE AUTHOR

Eric Butterworth has been a Unity minister for fifty years. He has lectured across the United States and Canada, and in Europe, South America, and Japan. He lives in Greenwich, Connecticut.